# THE TOWER *of London*

D1119664

# WHAT TO SEE

## THE CROWN JEWELS

**30 mins** The Tower of London has been home to the world famous British Crown Jewels since the beginning of the 14th century. Still used by The Queen and her family today, the Crown Jewels are an essential part of your visit to the Tower of London (see pages 22-25). See also the Martin Tower exhibition – *Crowns and Diamonds: the making of the Crown Jewels* – on the Wall Walk.

## THE WHITE TOWER

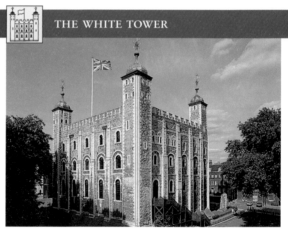

**30 mins** Begun in the reign of William the Conqueror (1066-87), the White Tower marks the start of the Tower of London's history as both a palace and a fortress. Today, it contains magnificent new displays of arms and armour from the collection of the Royal Armouries (see pages 32-37).

## WESTERN ENTRANCE & WATER LANE

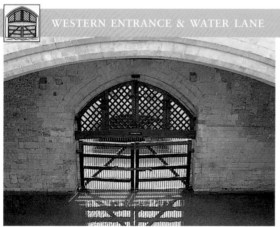

**30 mins** As you enter the Tower of London through the Middle and Byward towers, it is possible to get an impression of how the Tower was protected against potential attack. Walking along Water Lane you can also see Traitors' Gate where many famous prisoners entered the Tower of London for the last time. Other attractions include Henry III's Watergate and a torture display in the Lower Wakefield Tower (see pages 6-11).

## THE WALL WALK

**20 mins** The Tower of London is surrounded by a series of massive defensive walls. A walk around the eastern section provides an opportunity to see the Martin Tower exhibition – *Crowns and Diamonds: the making of the Crown Jewels* – and a model showing the Tower as it might have appeared in *c*1335 (see pages 18-21).

*The Tower of London has many important buildings and collections to explore and educational and entertaining events to take part in. This guide will help you plan your day.*

## THE MEDIEVAL PALACE

**30 mins** The Tower of London was a residence for the kings and queens of England as well as being a fortress. These rooms are shown as they might have appeared during the reign of Edward I (1272-1307). An exhibition about how the buildings were restored can be found inside (see pages 12-17).

## TOWER GREEN

**30 mins** Some of the Tower's most famous and important prisoners were held in the buildings around Tower Green including Sir Walter Ralegh who was imprisoned in the Bloody Tower for 13 years. In front of the Chapel Royal of St Peter ad Vincula seven famous prisoners were beheaded (see pages 26-31).

## THE FUSILIERS' MUSEUM

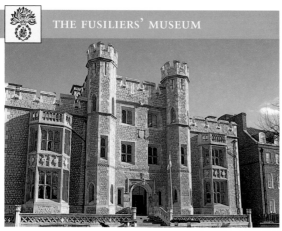

**20 mins** The Army has been involved with the Tower of London ever since its creation and today the Royal Regiment of Fusiliers, who were founded in 1685 to protect the royal guns within the Tower, open their museum to the public. On display are many fascinating exhibits that illustrate the history of the Regiment (see pages 38-39).

## THE YEOMAN WARDERS   **60 mins**

Yeoman Warders (often called 'Beefeaters') have been at the Tower of London since the 14th century. Today they combine their traditional ceremonial role with that of tourist guide. For details of their guided tours and talks (English only) and other free events today, see the Information Boards marked on your map.

## THE RAVENS   **15 mins**

Legend has it that Charles II was told that if the Ravens left the Tower, the kingdom would fall; so he ensured that a limited number would be kept here permanently. The story of the Ravens is told next to their lodgings.

## SPECIAL EVENTS

For details of today's special events, see the Information Boards – their locations are marked on your map.

# A GUIDE *to the Tower's*

*The Tower of London was begun in the reign of William the Conqueror (1066-87) and remained little changed for over a century. Then, between 1190 and 1285, the White Tower was encircled by two towered curtain walls and a great moat. The only important enlargement of the Tower after that time was the building of the Wharf, begun by Edward III (1327-77) and completed under Richard II (1377-99). To this day the medieval defences are essentially unchanged, except for the draining of the moat.*

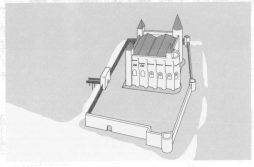

I. THE TOWER *c*1100

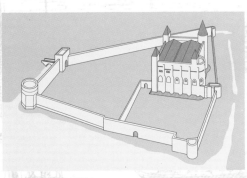

2. THE TOWER *c*1200

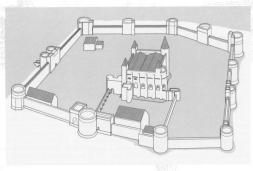

3. THE TOWER *c*1270

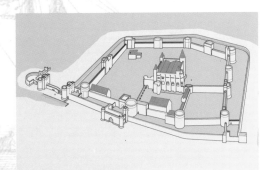

4. THE TOWER *c*1300

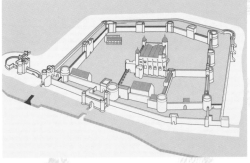

5. THE TOWER *c*1547

# development

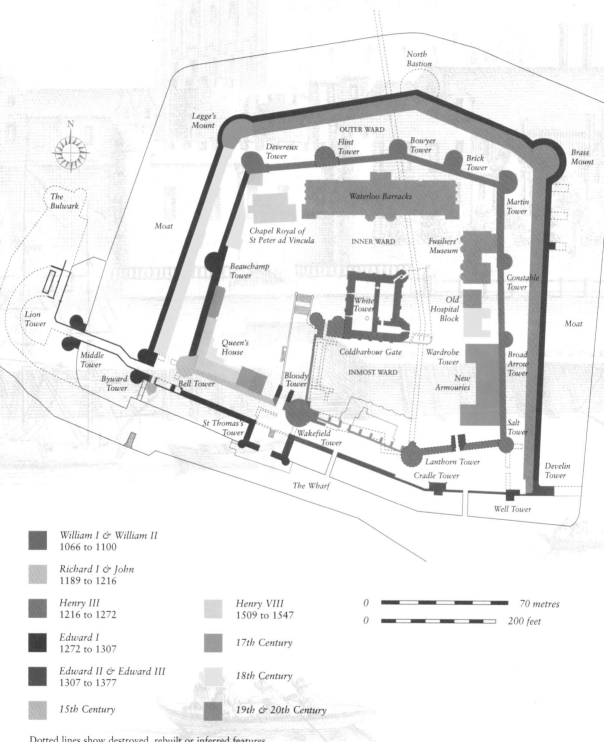

North
Bastion

Legge's
Mount

OUTER WARD

Devereux
Tower

Flint
Tower

Bowyer
Tower

Brick
Tower

Brass
Mount

The
Bulwark

Moat

Waterloo Barracks

Martin
Tower

Chapel Royal of
St Peter ad Vincula

INNER WARD

Fusiliers'
Museum

Constable
Tower

Beauchamp
Tower

White
Tower

Old
Hospital
Block

Lion
Tower

Moat

Middle
Tower

Queen's
House

Coldharbour Gate

Wardrobe
Tower

Broad
Arrow
Tower

Byward
Tower

Bell Tower

Bloody
Tower

INMOST WARD

New
Armouries

N

St Thomas's
Tower

Wakefield
Tower

Salt
Tower

Cradle Tower

Lanthorn Tower

Develin
Tower

The Wharf

Well Tower

William I & William II
1066 to 1100

Richard I & John
1189 to 1216

Henry III
1216 to 1272

Henry VIII
1509 to 1547

0 —————— 70 metres

Edward I
1272 to 1307

17th Century

0 —————— 200 feet

Edward II & Edward III
1307 to 1377

18th Century

15th Century

19th & 20th Century

Dotted lines show destroyed, rebuilt or inferred features

# WESTERN ENTRANCE & WATER LANE

*Watercolour of the Byward Tower by John Crowther, 1883.*

*This area extends from the western entrance of the Tower of London (the main visitor entrance) to the Cradle Tower at the end of Water Lane. It is suggested that you explore this area either as you arrive at or leave the Tower.*

## The Western Entrance

From the time of Edward I (1272-1307) the main entrance to the castle from the land was via a series of gatehouses and drawbridges that, due to later alterations, have today lost much of their impact. Edward I's expansion of the Tower included the construction of a new outer wall with main entrances both from the city and the river. The new and elaborate western entrance by land from the city was constructed between 1275 and 1281 and consisted of a barbican (outer defence), later called the Lion Tower and now demolished, and two twin-towered gatehouses, the Middle and Byward towers.

It is still possible to see the ancient drawbridge pit and the outer wall of the Lion Tower, the outline of which is marked out by stones set into the cobbles in front of the Tower Shop. It took its name from the Royal Menagerie, famous for its lions, which once occupied the tower. The Menagerie was only moved from the Lion Tower in 1834 (to form the nucleus of London Zoo) after which the tower was levelled and the building now used as the Tower Shop was built over it as a pumphouse.

*The interior of the Lion Tower in 1779 showing the animals' cages arranged around the perimeter of the tower with an exercise yard in the centre.*

*Main picture opposite: Traitors' Gate. Tradition holds that Princess Elizabeth (later Queen Elizabeth I) arrived at Traitors' Gate in 1554 and declared 'Here lands as true a subject, being prisoner, as ever landed at these stairs'.*

## The Middle Tower

From the Lion Tower a second drawbridge, also now destroyed, led to the Middle Tower which was constructed by Edward I but substantially altered and refaced in 1717, when the arms of George I were erected over the gate. It is now an office of the Royal Armouries. The entrance passage was originally defended by two portcullises, the grooves of which are still visible inside the archway.

*The Middle Tower, c1821. As its name suggests, the Middle Tower was positioned between the Byward Tower and the Lion Tower (now demolished).*

## The Byward Tower

A causeway, which originally contained a third drawbridge, leads from the Middle Tower to the Byward Tower (remember that until 1843 the moat was full of water). This gatehouse, with its two bold cylindrical towers, contains many original features from the time of Edward I. Like the Middle Tower, the Byward Tower was originally defended by two portcullises. Looking up on passing through the gateway you can see the surviving portcullis and a series of so-called 'murder holes', probably used to douse fires lit against the gates by intruders. The arrow loop on the right at the front of the gate passage is original and would have also been used to protect the gateway.

Just to the right of the gateway is a small postern gate, or private entrance, which gave access to the Tower from the Wharf (you can see the gateway and drawbridge to it from the Wharf) and was often used by royalty in the 15th and 16th centuries. This entrance was originally constructed by Edward II but its present form dates from the 15th century.

## Water Lane

After passing under the Byward Tower you enter Edward I's Outer Ward with Mint Street running north on your left and Water Lane ahead.

The Outer Ward was created by Edward I's expansion of the Tower in 1275-85 when a new outer curtain wall was constructed on the western, northern and eastern sides of the castle. The whole of the

*Water Lane looking west to the Bell Tower and the rear of the Byward Tower.*

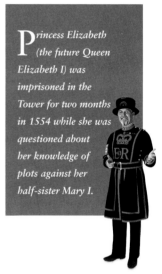

*Princess Elizabeth (the future Queen Elizabeth I) was imprisoned in the Tower for two months in 1554 while she was questioned about her knowledge of plots against her half-sister Mary I.*

Outer Ward along the south (the present Water Lane) was reclaimed from the river and a towered curtain wall constructed along the foreshore of the Thames. Before this time all the towers on the inner curtain wall stood on the river's edge, hence the name Water Lane.

Most of the area between the inner and outer curtain walls, from the Bell Tower round to the Salt Tower, was eventually occupied by the workshops, offices and houses of the Royal Mint which produced the country's currency. The section north of the Bell Tower is still known as Mint Street. Looking along Mint Street you can see the Casemates, a row of late 18th-century terraced cottages built against the rear of the outer curtain wall, where Yeomen Warders live with their families.

## The Bell Tower

The Bell Tower stands on the corner of Mint Street and Water Lane and is the oldest tower in the castle, other than the White Tower. The Bell Tower and the adjoining curtain wall, running along Water Lane to the Bloody Tower, date from an early enlargement of the Tower in the 1190s, at which time they stood on the edge of the river. You can see the Bell Tower's original plinth, once on the foreshore of the Thames, in a small railed-off pit beside the tower. The shape of the Bell Tower suggests it was probably built in two phases, the circular second storey being added at a later date to the lower polygonal plan. The curfew bell has been rung from this tower for at least 500 years although the present bell dates from 1651.

*The Bell Tower from the Wharf.*

*Sir Thomas More was imprisoned in the Bell Tower in 1534 for refusing to acknowledge Henry VIII as head of the English Church in place of the Pope. He was executed on Tower Hill in 1535.*

From very early in the Tower's history the Constable's residence adjoined the Bell Tower. Under the Tudors, when a major responsibility of the Constable's resident deputy, the Lieutenant, was the safekeeping of prisoners, the Bell Tower became the lodging of particularly important captives, such as Sir Thomas More and Bishop John Fisher.

As you walk along Water Lane, high above on the left-hand side is the rear of the present Queen's House where the Governor of the Tower still resides today. The entrance to the Medieval Palace (see page 13) is ahead on your right and just beyond is Traitors' Gate where the tour of Water Lane continues. The Bloody Tower gateway opposite leads into the Inner Ward.

*Cranmer at the Traitors' Gate by Frederick Goodall, 1856. Thomas Cranmer (1489-1556), Archbishop of Canterbury, was committed to the Tower in 1553 and charged with high treason for declaring Mary I illegitimate and supporting the attempt to place the Protestant Lady Jane Grey on the throne.*

## Traitors' Gate

St Thomas's Tower was built by Edward I between 1275 and 1279 to provide accommodation for the King and a new water entrance to the Tower, replacing Henry III's watergate of the Bloody Tower behind it. This river entrance is now often referred to as Traitors' Gate because of the number of prisoners accused of treason that are supposed to have passed through it. For prisoners such as Queen Anne Boleyn and Sir Thomas More the trip was to be their last.

In the pool behind Traitors' Gate was an engine that was used for raising water to a cistern on the roof of the White Tower. The engine worked originally by the force of the tide or by horsepower and eventually by steam. In 1724-6 it was adapted to drive machinery for boring gun barrels. It was removed in the 1860s.

*The timber framing above the great arch of Traitors' Gate is Tudor dating from 1532-3, although much restored in the 19th century.*

## Henry III's Watergate & Torture display

Continue along Water Lane, under the 19th-century bridge which links St Thomas's Tower to the Wakefield Tower, and on the left are the remains of Henry III's (1216-72) private watergate. This would originally have led from the river directly into the ground floor of the Wakefield Tower.

The lower chamber of the Wakefield Tower contained a guard room where the soldiers who guarded the watergate were stationed. This overlooked the river through a series of arrow slits, until about 1280 when the foreshore was built up to form the new Outer Ward. Today, the lower chamber contains replicas of three torture instruments, known to have been used at the Tower in past centuries. They comprise the infamous rack, the manacles and the Scavenger's Daughter, the latter designed by a former Lieutenant of the Tower. Interactive screens located near the Ravens' Lodgings provide more information on this theme. The upper chamber of the Wakefield Tower is open to the public as part of the Medieval Palace (see page 13).

As you leave the lower chamber of the Wakefield Tower turn left and pass under the Bloody Tower gateway that leads back into Water Lane.

*Twenty different masons' marks are preserved in the lower Wakefield Tower. These marks were used by masons on piecework to identify every stone that they had cut, so that the paymaster could calculate how much was due to them.*

## The Cradle Tower

Further along Water Lane stands the Cradle Tower, built by Edward III (1327-77) as a new private watergate to his own lodgings which were sited in and around the Lanthorn Tower. Inside you can see two guard chambers and the groove that originally housed the portcullis. The very handsome stone vault should also be noticed.

The Cradle Tower was later used as prison lodgings. In 1597 two prisoners managed to escape from the tower. Father John Gerard and John Arden swung to freedom on a rope stretched from the Cradle Tower across the moat where they were met by friends waiting in a boat.

Opposite the Cradle Tower is Queen Elizabeth II's Arch that leads into the Inner Ward.

*The Cradle Tower from Water Lane. During the 18th century the upper storey of the Cradle Tower was removed. It was rebuilt in c1868-9 by the architect Anthony Salvin.*

# THE MEDIEVAL PALACE

*The entrance to the Medieval Palace is in Water Lane, beside Traitors' Gate. A display about the history of the royal lodgings can be found inside.*

The group of buildings known today as the Medieval Palace give visitors an opportunity to see the part of the Tower of London that was generally used by the kings of England when in residence. The heart of what was formerly the residential quarter of the Tower is known as the Inmost Ward and this can be viewed from the south Wall Walk between the Wakefield and Lanthorn towers later in the tour.

## St Thomas's Tower

St Thomas's Tower was built by Edward I between 1275 and 1279 to perform a dual function, providing additional royal accommodation for the King but also creating a new watergate at which the King could arrive from the river. This is now known as Traitors' Gate because it was through here that prisoners accused of treason arrived from Westminster (see page 10).

St Thomas's Tower has been altered many times since it was first built and the first chamber has been left unrestored to show the extent of the archaeological evidence which survives from the many uses the tower has had since the 13th century.

In 1532, in preparation for the coronation of Henry VIII's second wife, Anne Boleyn, St Thomas's Tower was largely rebuilt to provide lodgings for high-ranking court officials. By the early 18th century, the condition

*Edward I surrounded by archbishops and clergy. This 13th-century manuscript illumination is the only surviving picture of Edward I in a medieval interior. Note the richness of the decoration and furniture.*

*Top right: Watercolour by John Crowther, 1883, showing (from left to right) the Bloody Tower, Wakefield Tower and St Thomas's Tower.*

*Main picture opposite: The upper chamber of the Wakefield Tower built for Henry III between 1220 and 1240.*

*Edward I and his wife, Eleanor of Castile. Edward I was a rare visitor to the Tower of London despite spending vast sums of money improving its accommodation and defences.*

of the tower had sadly deteriorated. Machinery for boring gun barrels (powered by an engine in the pool behind Traitors' Gate) was located inside the tower, but it also provided accommodation for the Keeper of the Engine, a number of Yeoman Warders and the patients of the Tower infirmary. In the 1860s the architect Anthony Salvin, was commissioned to carry out a major restoration of St Thomas's Tower and externally it remains as he left it. The tower became the residence of the Jewel House Keeper (the jewels then being housed in the adjoining Wakefield Tower) and later of the Deputy Governor of the Tower of London. It was only in the early 1990s that the tower was opened to the public.

In the 13th century, the first, unrestored, room was the King's Great Chamber. It was here that he had his bed, strongroom and garderobe (lavatory). Unfortunately, very little of this survives but you can visit his strongroom in the small turret which overlooks the river and see the remains of his garderobe next door to it. A model gives an impression of how the room might have looked in the reign of Edward I. Information panels identify original 13th-century features and others from later building works. The exhibition in the area created by the partition walls explains the philosophy behind the 1990s restoration.

The second room was originally the King's private hall and has been reconstructed using the kind of evidence still visible in the Great Chamber and other contemporary examples. This was where King Edward would have dined, entertained and prayed. In the small turret, which originally overlooked the Thames, but today looks out over the Wharf to Tower Bridge, is a small oratory (a room for prayer).

From St Thomas's Tower a covered bridge, built in the 19th century on the site of an earlier one, leads you to the Wakefield Tower.

*Above: The oratory in St Thomas's Tower and (right) the King's private hall, which has been reconstructed to show what the room might have looked like in the reign of Edward I (1272-1307).*

## The Wakefield Tower

This tower is the second largest in the Tower of London, after the White Tower. It was built between 1220 and 1240, in the reign of Henry III (1216-72) as an addition to the earlier palace buildings that he enlarged and improved. In addition to containing the King's principal private room it was also a strongpoint in the Tower's enlarged defences. Then standing directly on the river's edge, it commanded on one side what was then the main watergate (later incorporated into the Bloody Tower) and on the other side a small postern, the King's private entrance from the river, which you can see in Water Lane. From Water Lane you can also visit the lower chamber of the Wakefield Tower, which contains a display about torture at the Tower (see page 11).

The upper chamber of the Wakefield Tower, with its vaulted ceiling (a 19th-century reconstruction), large windows and fireplace was built to be the private chamber or bedchamber of Henry III (his bed may have occupied the square niche to the north east). At that time it would have given access to a private hall to the west, where the King would meet his council and dine publicly, and beyond that to the great hall – the heart of the palace – that extended as far as the Lanthorn Tower.

*The Wakefield Tower provided royal accommodation for Henry III and his son, Edward I. It later became a repository for documents, a use that continued up to the 19th century when it was converted to house the Crown Jewels.*

The interior has now been furnished to evoke its appearance in the time of Edward I on the evidence of written accounts and comparable interiors and furniture surviving from the period. Under Edward I this room lost its original function as a bedchamber, and became an ante-room to the new chambers in St Thomas's Tower. As such, it may have been used as a presence chamber or throne room and today a throne, copied from the Coronation Chair in Westminster Abbey, occupies an embrasure on the west side. After Edward's death in 1307, the king's private chamber was moved to the area of the Lanthorn Tower and the Wakefield Tower was abandoned as a residence.

*The Wakefield Tower housed the Crown Jewels for almost 100 years. This engraving shows the jewels on display in c1875.*

Behind the painted timber screen is a small chapel lit by a stained-glass window and equipped with a *sedilia* (a seat for the priest), a piscina, the basin in which the vessels for Mass were washed (on the right), and an aumbry, or wall cupboard (on the left) in which they were stored. The screen is copied from a mid-13th-century example in Oxfordshire.

By tradition, the chapel is particularly associated with Henry VI (1422-61 and 1470-1) who was taken prisoner in 1471 by the new Yorkist King, Edward IV, during the Wars of the Roses, when two branches of the royal house of Plantagenet (the Lancastrians and Yorkists) fought for the throne. Henry was reputedly lodged in the Wakefield Tower and shortly after murdered whilst at prayer, possibly on Edward's order. But in fact, long before Henry VI's imprisonment the Wakefield Tower had become a storehouse for official documents, and it is more likely that he was imprisoned in the Lanthorn Tower where the King's lodgings were. When the official records were moved to the new Public Record Office in Chancery Lane, which opened in 1856, the upper Wakefield Tower housed the Crown Jewels until a new Jewel House opened in 1967. This Jewel House was in its turn replaced by the existing Jewel House in 1994.

You leave the Wakefield Tower by a spiral staircase that takes you up on to the south Wall Walk.

## The Wall Walk

*The Record Office in the Wakefield Tower by Charles Tomkins, 1801. In the cupboards, or presses, you can see rows of medieval documents.*

This stretch of wall, which runs to the Lanthorn Tower, is a very good place from which to understand the layout of the Inmost Ward. Today this open grass area bears little relation to any earlier period in Tower history than about 1900, but it was, in fact, included in the very first enclosure of the castle. To the east (right) of the White Tower marked out on the grass is the line of the Roman wall, built in about A.D. 200 together with the foundation of a Roman bastion added to it around A.D. 400 on which the Wardrobe Tower was built in the 11th century. Further on, directly beneath the Wall Walk on which you are standing is a section of the riverside city wall of around A.D. 390 that is exposed and can be seen in front of the Medieval Palace Shop. The White Tower was originally built inside these stretches of Roman wall, and the northern and western sides of the enclosure in which it stood was closed off by a ditch and an earth and timber rampart. These defences were later improved and eventually the area in front of the White Tower was closed off by a massive gatehouse erected in the 13th century at the south-west corner of the White Tower, the foundations of which can be still seen to its left. This was called the Coldharbour Gate and provided access into the Inmost Ward of the castle. Running between this and the Wakefield Tower are the remains of the wall that provided defence on the west of the Inmost Ward. A series of arrow slits still survive. The area thus enclosed contained the king's great hall, his kitchen and, much later, a range of buildings specially erected for the coronation of Henry VIII's second wife, Anne Boleyn.

Later the palace was enlarged: Henry VIII built a jewel house against the south face of the White Tower (facing the river) and an annexe on its eastern side, and eventually a second palace precinct was formed between the Lanthorn Tower and the Wardrobe Tower on the west, and the Salt Tower and Broad Arrow Tower on the east. The medieval buildings survived long after royalty had ceased to use the palace. Some were demolished in 1674-5 and others, including the great hall, were incorporated into new storehouses and offices, which in turn were pulled down in 1775-7 as a result of the fire that destroyed the Lanthorn Tower.

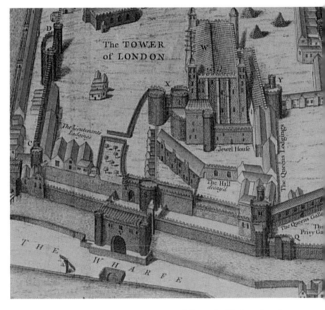

## The Lanthorn Tower

The original Lanthorn Tower, built at the same time as the Wakefield Tower for the queen's residence, was gutted by fire in 1774 and soon after demolished. The present building was reconstructed in the late 19th century and today contains a number of 13th-century artefacts which illustrate life in the palace of Edward I.

As you leave the Lanthorn Tower, before exiting down the Queen Elizabeth II steps, several important towers can be seen from the Wall Walk. Looking towards Tower Bridge, the furthest tower to the east (left), standing at the south-east corner of the Outer Ward, is the Develin Tower. At one period a causeway ran from this tower across the moat forming a back entrance (or postern) to the castle. To the right of the Develin Tower is the low, block-like Well Tower, perhaps the only tower other than the White Tower to have kept its medieval name, for though it did not have a well, its outer walls contained chutes down which buckets were lowered into the river. Next along, and almost opposite the Lanthorn Tower, is the Cradle Tower, built by Edward III (1372-7) as the new water entrance to the King's chambers, by then in the Lanthorn Tower. The Cradle Tower is open to the public and can be visited from Water Lane (see page 11).

*Detail from the Haiward and Gascoyne survey of the Tower of London of 1597 (as engraved in 1742) showing the Medieval Palace complex (V = St Thomas's Tower, S = the Wakefield Tower, R = the Lanthorn Tower). Note the ruins of the great hall (marked 'decay'd'), by then without a roof.*

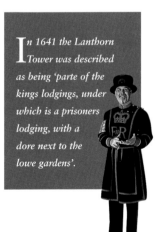

In 1641 the Lanthorn Tower was described as being 'parte of the kings lodgings, under which is a prisoners lodging, with a dore next to the lowe gardens'.

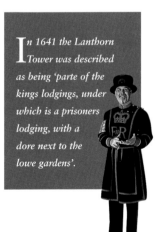

# THE WALL WALK

*Illustration of about 1300, depicting the legendary siege of the Tower of London by Mordred, rebel son of King Arthur. The depiction of the castle is fanciful, but shows methods of attack and defence current c1250-1350.*

*Access to the Wall Walk is via the Salt Tower in the Inner Ward. The exhibition **Crowns and Diamonds: the making of the Crown Jewels** is located in the Martin Tower at the end of the Wall Walk.*

The Wall Walk takes visitors round the towers along the east side of the castle from the Salt Tower to the Martin Tower. Most of it, including eight wall towers, was built in the later years of Henry III's reign from 1238 onwards, though his son, Edward I, reconstructed the western section, which includes the Beauchamp Tower, beginning in 1275. The Inner Ward comprises the area within the inner curtain wall (except for the Inmost Ward to the south of the White Tower).

The building of this towered curtain wall transformed the defences of the Tower of London. Archers and missile-throwing machines along the walls, and on and within the towers that projected from them, had a good command of the land around the castle and could concentrate projectiles against an attack at any point. If the enemy managed to get on to or over the wall, they were still exposed to missiles from the adjoining mural towers as well as from the White Tower.

Like most English castles, the Tower was rarely under attack and in peaceful times the wall towers were used for domestic rather than military purposes. Each tower contains two or three floors, with a sizeable chamber on each. Together these might form a suite of rooms for a resident or guest of the highest rank, accompanied by his own household, or the rooms might be arranged as self-contained accommodation. Later on the towers were easily adapted to hold prisoners. Some were kept in one room, either in solitary confinement or together with their accomplices. Others, more favourably treated because of their high rank, were allowed servants and allotted an entire tower.

The inscriptions in the Wall Walk towers include those of Ambrose Rookewoode (Martin Tower) and Sir Everard Digby (Broad Arrow Tower), two of the conspirators in the Gunpowder Plot who were held at the Tower before being executed in 1606.

*Main picture opposite: The Martin Tower was used as prison lodgings before being converted into the Jewel House in 1669. It was from here that 'Colonel' Thomas Blood made his daring attempt to steal the Crown Jewels in 1671.*

The Salt Tower

The first tower on the Wall Walk is the Salt Tower. The ground floor is typical of many of these towers and would have been used for storage in peaceful times. When there was trouble, archers would have been able to protect the walls of the castle at low level by shooting through the arrow loops within the embrasures.

More loops appear in the first floor chamber together with a large window with fine tracery that would have originally overlooked the river and was, therefore, not vulnerable to attack from the land. This chamber also contains a fine original hooded fireplace and, beyond the staircase that leads out of the tower, a garderobe (lavatory), two essential features of a chamber fit for an occupant of high status. Indeed, one of the earliest residents in the Salt Tower, between 1296 and 1299, was John Baliol, previously King of Scotland (1292-6), who had surrendered his crown to Edward I following defeat in battle. In the Tudor period, this room was in constant use as a prison cell, and many Catholic priests were held here during the reign of Elizabeth I (1558-1603). You can see some of their inscriptions carved into the walls during their imprisonment, including that of the English Jesuit priest, Henry Walpole (1558-95).

*Watercolour by J.W. Archer, 1846, showing the demolition of the Golden Chain Tavern and part of Henry III's curtain wall adjacent to the Salt Tower. Once this work was complete the Salt Tower was found to be in need of repair and was subsequently restored by Anthony Salvin in 1857-8.*

From the Salt Tower the Wall Walk continues to the Broad Arrow Tower. Looking down over the wall, some of the Yeoman Warders' houses can be seen, built in the 1860s by Anthony Salvin and still used for their original purpose today. The brick building running along the left side of the wall is the rear of the New Armouries building.

*John Baliol (1249-1315) the Scottish King (seen here with his wife Isabella) was imprisoned in the Salt Tower by Edward I. He was released after three years and banished to France.*

*Two inscriptions attributed to one of Princess Elizabeth's tutors, Giovanni Battista Castiglione, from the Salt Tower (top) and Broad Arrow Tower.*

The Broad Arrow Tower

From the 14th century the Broad Arrow Tower was associated with the Wardrobe, a department of government responsible for royal supplies. The tower takes its name from the broad arrow that was stamped on goods to show their royal ownership. In later years the tower became a prison and contains many inscriptions made by prisoners who were held here in the 16th and 17th centuries. To the left of the fireplace is an inscription attributed to Giovanni Battista Castiglione, the Italian tutor of Princess Elizabeth, later Queen Elizabeth I, who was held here during the Protestant uprisings in the reign of her half-sister, Queen Mary I.

The Wall Walk between the Broad Arrow Tower and the Constable Tower runs along behind the Hospital Block and the back of the Headquarters of the Royal Regiment of Fusiliers.

## The Constable Tower

The Constable Tower houses a model showing the Tower of London as it might have appeared in *c*1335 during the reign of Edward III.

## The Martin Tower

For 200 years this tower was known as the Jewel Tower because, from 1669, it was where the Crown Jewels were displayed. The jewels were housed on the ground floor while the upper rooms became the residence of the Keeper of the Regalia.

*The Crown Jewels on display in the lower Martin Tower, c1820. In 1841 the jewels had to be hurriedly removed from the Martin Tower as fire raged through the Grand Storehouse next door.*

Today the Martin Tower houses an exhibition – *Crowns and Diamonds: the making of the Crown Jewels* – which traces the development of English royal crowns and tells the story of some of their most famous stones. On display are the frames of the coronation crowns worn by George IV (1821), Queen Adelaide (1831) and Queen Alexandra (1902) and the state crowns made for George I (1715) and Queen Victoria (1838). Further information about this exhibition can be found in the Crown Jewels guidebook.

The first Keeper of the Regalia in the Martin Tower was one Talbot Edwards who died in September 1674 and was buried in the Chapel Royal of St Peter ad Vincula on Tower Green. His memorial stone can be seen on the south wall of the Chapel.

The next stretch of Wall Walk along the north side of the Inner Ward incorporates four further towers, currently not open to the public. The Brick Tower, Flint Tower and the upper storey of the Bowyer Tower were rebuilt in the 19th century after being damaged by the fire that destroyed the Grand Storehouse in 1841. In the Bowyer Tower, it is traditionally believed that George Duke of Clarence, a brother of Edward IV, was privately executed in 1478 by drowning in a butt of his favourite malmsey wine (Maderia) after his conviction for treason.

The Devereux Tower, confronting the troublesome City of London at the north-west corner of the Inner Ward, is of exceptional strength. When the castle was threatened by Protestant rebels under Sir Thomas Wyatt in 1554, guns mounted on the roof of the Devereux Tower were fired on the city.

After leaving the Martin Tower visitors descend to the Inner Ward by a staircase. The lower floor of the Martin Tower contains the Jewel House Shop.

*George IV's Coronation Crown set with over 12,000 diamonds and other precious stones for his coronation in 1821.*

# THE CROWN JEWELS

*The Jewel House is in the Waterloo Barracks in the Inner Ward. Entrance is via the main central door. Once inside the Jewel House you pass through a series of introductory areas that illustrate the use and history of the jewels, and include footage of the coronation of Her Majesty Queen Elizabeth II in 1953, before reaching the Treasury where the Crown Jewels are held.*

The Crown Jewels have been on public display at the Tower of London since the 17th century in a number of locations including the Martin Tower and the Wakefield Tower. Today they are housed in the Waterloo Barracks, which was built in the 19th century in a castellated neo-Gothic style complete with elaborate battlements and gargoyles. It was built while the Duke of Wellington was Constable of the Tower (1826-52) to provide accommodation for almost 1,000 soldiers.

*The Crown Jewels have been held at the Tower of London since the 14th century, except for the period of the Second World War when they were moved to a secret location before being returned to the Tower in 1945.*

*Engraving of the Waterloo Barracks in the mid-19th century. The statue of the Duke of Wellington in the foreground was erected shortly after the building was completed. It was later moved to the Royal Arsenal at Woolwich where it remains to this day.*

*Top right: Her Majesty Queen Elizabeth II wearing the Imperial State Crown and holding the Sovereign's Orb and Sceptre on the day of her coronation, 2 June 1953.*

*Main picture opposite: St Edward's Crown, 1661.*

23

*Charles II by John Michael Wright, c1661.*
*Although Charles II's state crown no longer*
*survives, the orb and sceptre made for the*
*King in 1661 have been used at every*
*subsequent coronation.*

The jewels on display in the Jewel House are largely those items used at the coronation of a sovereign and are collectively known as the Coronation Regalia. Most of the collection dates from the restoration of the monarchy in 1660, when Charles II ascended the throne. The old regalia used up to the coronation of the last king, Charles I, in 1626 had been destroyed after his execution in 1649 when Oliver Cromwell, the Parliamentary general, ordered that it be 'totally broken, and that they melt down all the gold and silver, and sell the jewels to the best advantage of the Commonwealth'. Today only three swords and the Coronation Spoon pre-date Charles II's time.

Some of the new regalia made for Charles II, such as the Sovereign's Orb and Sceptre, have been used at every subsequent coronation including the coronation of Her Majesty Queen Elizabeth II in 1953. There have also been many additions and alterations to the regalia since Charles II's day. For example, a new set of regalia had to be made in 1685 for Mary of Modena, James II's wife, as she was the first queen consort to be crowned with her husband since the Restoration. Another new set was required in 1689 for Mary II when she was crowned with her husband, William III, because she was queen in her own right and not queen consort.

*The Sovereign's Orb (left),*
*made for the coronation of*
*Charles II in 1661, and Queen*
*Mary II's Orb, 1689. The orb*
*represents sovereign power;*
*the cross on top symbolising*
*Christian rule.*

*From left to right: The Queen*
*Consort's Sceptre with Cross, 1685;*
*the Sovereign's Sceptre with Dove,*
*1661; Queen Mary II's Sceptre*
*with Dove, 1689 and the Queen*
*Consort's Ivory Rod with Dove,*
*1685.*

*The Imperial State Crown was made for the coronation of George VI in 1937 and altered for Her Majesty Queen Elizabeth II in 1953. It is set with 2,868 diamonds, 17 sapphires, 11 emeralds, 5 rubies and 273 pearls.*

In addition to their enormous historical value, the Crown Jewels incorporate some spectacular and priceless stones. The largest top quality cut diamond in the world, the First Star of Africa (Cullinan I), which weighs just over 530 carats, is set in the head of the Sovereign's Sceptre with Cross. Some stones are also famous for their historical associations and numerous legends surround the Koh-i-Noor diamond, set in the Crown of Queen Elizabeth The Queen Mother and the 'Stuart Sapphire', the 'Black Prince's Ruby' and 'Queen Elizabeth's Pearls', all set in the Imperial State Crown.

As well as the Coronation Regalia, the Jewel House also contains a number of crowns not associated with the coronation ceremony, christening fonts, altar plate and banqueting plate including the magnificent Wine Cistern which is said to be the heaviest recorded surviving piece of English plate weighing over 248 kilograms.

The Crown Jewels have not always been as securely held as they are today. In 1671, when the jewels were housed in the Martin Tower, 'Colonel' Thomas Blood made a daring attempt to steal the crown, orb and sceptre and got as far as Tower Wharf before he and his accomplices were caught. In 1815, a madwoman got hold of the State Crown and wrenched its arches apart causing considerable damage. In 1841 a serious fire again threatened their safety.

Today the Martin Tower houses the Jewel House Shop and an exhibition *Crowns and Diamonds: the making of the Crown Jewels*. An illustrated guidebook to the Crown Jewels is on sale in all the Tower shops.

*This magnificent altar dish dates from 1664 and is decorated with a representation of the Last Supper. Measuring some 37.5" (94.6cm) in diameter, it is one of the largest surviving altar dishes of the period.*

# TOWER GREEN

*Tower Green is in the south-west corner of the Inner Ward which is entered from Water Lane. It has been an area of garden for probably 300 years and is bounded on its south and west by a range of buildings that have traditionally accommodated Tower of London officials, and still do today.*

*Right: The Bloody Tower from the north by Frederick Nash, 1821. In 1603 the Bloody Tower was heightened and a new floor inserted to provide more space for Sir Walter Ralegh and his family.*

## The Bloody Tower

Before the building of St Thomas's Tower, the tower that came to be called the Bloody Tower stood on the edge of the river and controlled the main river entrance to the castle. After 1280, with the construction of the Outer Ward and the new watergate of St Thomas's, it became the principal access from the Outer Ward to the Inner Ward.

The Bloody Tower was built in the early 1220s but the upper stage of the present tower was largely reconstructed in about 1360 during the reign of Edward III. The vaulted gate passage beneath the tower was originally defended by two gates and two portcullises, one of each at either end. Only the portcullis and gate at the south end survive today, complete with the windlass that operates the portcullis from the first floor.

*Main picture opposite: The Queen's House was where many distinguished prisoners were held including, by tradition, Henry VIII's second wife, Anne Boleyn. The last prisoner to stay in the Queen's House was Rudolf Hess, the Deputy Führer of Nazi Germany, who was held here for four days in May 1941.*

*The lower chamber of the Bloody Tower was intended to provide high quality accommodation. It contains a good fireplace, a large side window which once had window seats, and a floor of richly decorated tiles (now protected by matting).*

The lower chamber of the Bloody Tower was built as superior accommodation, perhaps a guest room or office, for the use of the Constable who lived nearby. Eventually this tower was to accommodate such eminent prisoners as two Archbishops of Canterbury, Thomas Cranmer (in 1553-4), and William Laud (in 1640-5), and a Lord Chancellor, Judge Jeffreys (in 1688-9). Accommodation for important or high-ranking prisoners such as these, which reflected their status and enabled them to live with their families, was not uncommon at the Tower.

### Sir Walter Ralegh

The Bloody Tower is now furnished as it might have appeared during the 13-year imprisonment (1603-16) of Sir Walter Ralegh who was charged with plotting against King James I. During his imprisonment, Ralegh wrote *The History of the World* (published 1614) and conducted many scientific experiments. He grew tobacco and other exotic plants and produced medicinal cordials.

*Sir Walter Ralegh (1552?-1618)*

### The Princes in the Tower

The tower was once known as the Garden Tower as it adjoined the Lieutenant's garden. At some time in the Tudor period it became known as the Bloody Tower because (or, so James I was told when he visited the Tower in 1604) it was where the 'Princes in the Tower' had been murdered.

*The Princes in the Tower, depicted by the Victorian artist John Millais. Although the princes are traditionally believed to have been imprisoned and murdered in the Bloody Tower, it is more likely that the boys were held in the White Tower.*

The princes, 12-year-old Edward and his younger brother, Richard, sons of Edward IV, had been lodged in the Tower following their father's death in 1483, under the protection of their uncle, Richard Duke of Gloucester. Preparations began for Edward's coronation but in the event it was their uncle who was crowned in his place as Richard III. The princes remained in the Tower for a time and then disappeared from view. Much has been written about their fate, mainly in order to prove or disprove Richard's involvement in their deaths, but no conclusive evidence has been produced. Even the bones of two children found buried close to the White Tower in 1674, which were officially reburied in Westminster Abbey as the remains of the princes, cannot be positively identified.

There have, however, been two authenticated cases of violent death within the Bloody Tower. In 1585 the 8th Earl of Northumberland shot himself to escape conviction for treason and the forfeiture of his family lands to Elizabeth I. In James I's reign, in scandalous circumstances that touched the King himself, Sir Thomas Overbury was poisoned while a prisoner here.

## The Queen's House

The Queen's House (the black and white timber-framed building next to the Bloody Tower) is the home of the Resident Governor of the Tower of London and is not open to the public. When it was first built it was known as the Lieutenant's Lodging after the Constable's deputy at the Tower, the Lieutenant. Its present name, Queen's House, dates from Queen Victoria's reign and changes according to whether the sovereign is king or queen.

Many prisoners of high rank were lodged here, under the personal supervision of the Lieutenant. In 1605 Guy Fawkes was interrogated in the Council Chamber, on the upper floor, both before and after torture. He was convicted of participating in the Gunpowder Plot, which had attempted to blow up James I and his Parliament, and was later executed. In 1608 an elaborate memorial was erected in the Council Chamber to commemorate the discovery of the plot.

One prisoner in the Lieutenant's care managed to escape from the Queen's House on the eve of his execution. The Scottish Earl of Nithsdale, captured after the defeat of the 1715 Jacobite Rebellion (which had attempted to overthrow George I), escaped rouged and in women's clothing which had been smuggled in by his wife.

On the left of the Queen's House are two 19th-century Yeoman Warder's houses and on the right are two small houses dating from the 17th century, originally built as residences for Tower officials, a function they still perform.

> Tower Green is the setting for many of the Tower's traditional ceremonies including state parades, the swearing-in of new Yeoman Warders and the Installation of the Constable, a ceremony that takes place every five years when a new Constable of the Tower is appointed.

## The Beauchamp Tower

The Beauchamp Tower was built by Edward I in about 1281, replacing the twin-towered gatehouse of Henry III's time that had controlled the landward entrance to his castle across the moat, and incorporating its foundations. The tower takes its name from Thomas Beauchamp, Earl of Warwick, who was imprisoned here by Richard II from 1397 to 1399.

Because of its ample accommodation and its close proximity to the Constable or his deputy residing where the Queen's House now stands, the Beauchamp Tower was especially suitable for prisoners of high rank. In Mary I's reign (1553-8), John Dudley, Duke of Northumberland, and his five sons were held here; in Elizabeth I's reign (1558-1603), Philip Howard, Earl of Arundel, died within its walls and here Lord Cobham spent the last 14 years of his life in the reign of James I (1603-25).

The upper chamber contains many inscriptions carved into the walls by prisoners who were held here. Most date from between 1532 and 1672. They vary from simple names and initials to elaborate bas-relief carvings, such as the coat of arms, floral border and poem by John Dudley (pictured right, top). The Yeoman Warder on duty can provide more information about them.

*Most of the inscriptions in the Beauchamp Tower were carved between 1532 and 1672.*

The extensive use of brick inside the Beauchamp Tower is a significant feature of Edward I's work at the Tower of London and, on this scale, an innovation in English castle-building.

Along the western curtain wall from the Devereux Tower to the Bell Tower, via the Beauchamp Tower, ran a continuous line of embrasures and arrow slits through which archers could defend the castle walls. Originally these were in the first line of defence, but after the outer curtain wall was built and subsequently heightened, they were retained to cover the Outer Ward.

On your left as you leave the Beauchamp Tower are two 18th-century houses built and used as residences for Tower officials. Today they are occupied by the resident Chaplain and Doctor of the Tower.

## The Scaffold Site

In front of the Chapel Royal of St Peter ad Vincula scaffolds were erected for the execution of seven famous prisoners.

The first was William, Lord Hastings, in 1483 hurriedly beheaded after his arrest at a meeting of the royal council at the Tower on the orders of the Protector, Richard Duke of Gloucester. The next five victims were the only women to suffer death by beheading for treason. Anne Boleyn (1536) and Catherine Howard (1542), Henry VIII's second and fifth wives, had both been convicted of adultery. Jane, Viscountess Rochford, Catherine's lady-in-waiting, was implicated in her crime and was executed with her. The aged Margaret Pole, Countess of Salisbury, was 70 when she was executed in 1541 by order of Henry VIII who saw her Yorkist blood and loyalty to Rome as a threat to his rule. Similarly, Lady Jane Grey, who was proclaimed queen upon the death of Edward VI in 1553, in an attempt to secure a Protestant succession, was executed in 1554 by her Catholic cousin, Mary I, who claimed the throne a few days into Jane's reign.

*Anne Boleyn (1507-36)*

*Catherine Howard (d.1542)*

*The Scaffold Site and, beyond, the Chapel Royal of St Peter ad Vincula where those who died on Tower Green are buried.*

These private executions that took place on Tower Green were intended to avoid embarrassing the prisoner as well as the monarch; the customary place for beheadings being outside the castle walls on Tower Hill, where thousands of unruly spectators turned out to watch.

The last of the seven, Robert Devereux, Earl of Essex, the young favourite of Elizabeth I, was also granted a private execution, probably for the same reason. However, Essex was also very popular with the people of London and when he fell from favour in 1601 the Queen's ministers feared what might happen if he were taken out to be executed among the crowds on Tower Hill.

# The Chapel Royal of St Peter ad Vincula

*Visitors are welcome to join one of the services in the Chapel (the sign outside provides details). At other times you may only enter the Chapel with a Yeoman Warder's tour (see your map for starting point) or after 4.30pm.*

The Chapel Royal of St Peter ad Vincula, close by the scaffold site, is the last resting place of all those who died there and also of many who died on Tower Hill. The dedication to St Peter 'in chains' suggests a special association with prisoners but long predates the time when the Tower came into regular use as a prison. St Peter's had been a city parish church standing outside the walls of the Tower until it was incorporated into the castle when it was enlarged by Henry III. He had the Chapel richly furnished and decorated as the place of worship for the community within the Tower, a role it still fulfils today.

*The Chapel is a rare example of early Tudor church architecture, consisting of a nave and chancel and an equally wide north aisle, with a roof of Spanish chestnut.*

St Peter's was rebuilt in the reign of Henry III's son, Edward I, and again rebuilt in its present form in 1519-20 in the early years of Henry VIII's reign.

The Chapel contains some splendid monuments commemorating officers of the Tower, their wives and families as well as memorials to many humble residents of the Tower who worshipped in this their parish church.

The Chapel is perhaps best known for being the burial place of some of the most famous Tower prisoners including three queens: Anne Boleyn, Catherine Howard and Jane Grey – and many others of noble blood or high position including two saints of the Roman Catholic Church, Sir Thomas More and Bishop John Fisher. At the time, their headless bodies were buried quickly and carelessly under the nave or chancel without any memorial. When, with Queen Victoria's approval, the Chapel was restored in 1876, the remains unearthed in the nave, along with some intact coffins, were re-interred in the crypt. Bones found in the chancel, some of which could be identified, including the remains of Anne Boleyn, were reburied beneath the marble pavement in front of the altar. The fine organ, built by Bernhardt Schmidt for the Banqueting House at Whitehall in 1699 and decorated with carvings by Grinling Gibbons, was installed in 1890. It was restored in 1999. In 1966, a professional choir was formed which has won an excellent reputation.

*One of the oldest memorials in the Chapel is the tomb of Sir Richard Cholmondeley (above) who was Lieutenant of the Tower during the reign of Henry VIII. In the event, he fell from favour and was not allowed to be buried in the Chapel.*

# THE WHITE TOWER

*The White Tower is the most imposing and historic building in the whole fortress. It now contains displays from the Royal Armouries' collection, telling the story of the building, as well as of arms and armour at the Tower.*

*The White Tower, showing the south-east apsidal protrusion which houses the east end of the Chapel.*

The White Tower has given its name to the entire castle – the Tower of London. Looking at the building today, dominating the entire site as it always has, it is easy to see why.

## The Exterior

The White Tower is the oldest medieval building at the Tower of London. It was put up within a slightly earlier fortified enclosure created by William the Conqueror (1066-87). The exact date at which building began is unknown but is traditionally given as 1078; certainly it was started during the reign of the Conqueror. It may have been the work of Gundulf, Bishop of Rochester, a renowned builder of castles and churches.

A massive rectangular tower: 35.9m (118ft) by 32.6m (107ft) across and 27.4m (90ft) high, the White Tower was intended to impress, but was also equipped as a fortress and a residence, providing accommodation for the King himself. As such it belongs to a class of buildings usually referred to as the 'keep', of which large numbers survive in England and in other parts of Europe – Dover (Kent) and Falaise in Normandy being famous examples. The White Tower is, however, the oldest and largest building of this type in England and was used as a model, endlessly adapted, for later structures.

*In the White Tower in 1399 King Richard II (1377-99) was condemned as a tyrant and forced to abdicate by his cousin, Henry of Bolingbroke, who became King Henry IV (1399-1413).*

*Main picture opposite: The White Tower from the south west showing the original (but now externally much altered) entrance at ground-floor level.*

*Engraving of the White Tower from the north east in 1821, showing the great annexe attributed to Edward III (1327-77) and demolished only in the 19th century.*

The origin of its own design is something of a puzzle. Sheer scale and quality apart, its main peculiarity is the apsidal (semi-circular) protrusion at its south-east corner which houses the east end of the Chapel. This feature is shared in England only by the 'keep' at Colchester (Essex). Either its builders were particularly innovative or, as now seems likely, they were following a model that had already long existed in Normandy, William the Conqueror's homeland.

Since the 11th century the exterior of the building has been much altered and repaired, although its basic form remains intact. Medieval work was largely confined to maintenance, although we know that Henry III (1216-72) refurbished the Chapel and had the outside of the building whitewashed, a procedure that gave the White Tower its name; the roof was completely replaced in 1490 at a higher level than previously. In later centuries much of the original cut stone from Caen in Normandy was replaced by more durable material from Portland (Dorset), so that little except the rubble walling remains from the 11th century. Most of the windows and door surrounds were replaced in the 17th and 18th centuries, and new entrances inserted; the Chapel windows were restored in a Romanesque style in 1864. Only four windows (top level at the left, facing the river) retain more or less their original shape. The ornate turret roofs date from the 16th century. Originally they were probably pyramidal.

*On the south face of the White Tower are four original windows which survive (although restored) from the Norman period.*

During the course of its history numerous buildings have been put up against the White Tower, including a wall linking it to the Wardrobe Tower (dating from about 1100), the 13th-century Coldharbour gatehouse to the south west (the remains can still be seen) and a huge annexe to the east (built in the 14th century and heightened in the early 19th century). This annexe was demolished only in 1879, leaving the White Tower freestanding, as its builders had intended.

The entrance to the White Tower is through the doorway (now much altered) on the south face, which was protected from attack by being raised well above ground level; it would have been reached by a timber stair, as it is today. In the 12th century a stone 'fore-building', containing a stone stair, was added at this point for extra protection. It was demolished in 1674.

*The four weather vanes on the turrets of the White Tower date from 1669.*

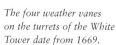

## The Interior

The White Tower in its present form contains three floors with a basement below, each split in two by a wall running north-south, the south-east quadrant being taken up by the Chapel and the spaces below it.

### The Basement

The basement of the White Tower was intended for storage and originally could only be reached from the floor above. Its two main rooms once had timber ceilings but were vaulted in brick in 1733 when the basement was used as a gunpowder store. The basement also contains the 11th-century well, 12m (40ft) deep, which was essential if the keep was to sustain a siege. It still contains fresh water. The western chamber houses the White Tower Shop.

*The second floor of the White Tower in 1863 showing elaborate displays of weaponry.*

*Henry VIII in jousting armour. Early in his reign the King brought French, Italian and German craftsmen over to England to work in the royal armour workshop in Greenwich.*

### The Ground Floor

The ground floor of the White Tower houses an exhibition from the collection of the Royal Armouries showing the history of displaying small arms at the Tower of London. The Royal Armouries derives from the great arsenal at the Tower that supplied armour and weapons to the medieval English kings and their armies. The present collection took shape in the reign of Henry VIII (1509-47) who re-stocked the Tower arsenal, and also set up a workshop at Greenwich to make fine armour for himself and his court. The exhibition also includes a model of the 17th-century Grand Storehouse (destroyed by fire in 1841), which housed magnificent displays of arms and armour.

Many original features survive in the room; note in particular the gigantic window embrasures and the original 11th-century round-backed fireplace. At this level the space under the Chapel is occupied by a barrel-vaulted room with south and east-facing windows.

It is thought that the two main rooms on this floor were originally occupied by the Constable (the monarch's deputy at the Tower) or may have served as ceremonial reception rooms for the king himself.

The first recorded prisoner at the Tower of London was Ranulf Flambard, Bishop of Durham, who was imprisoned in the White Tower in 1100 on the orders of Henry I. In 1101 he managed to escape, using a rope smuggled to him in a pot of wine, and fled to Normandy.

## The First Floor

Two spiral stairs lead to the next floor, the main one being housed in the massive round turret at the north-east corner – placed as far away as possible from the main entrance to hinder intruders. The basic layout mirrors that of the floor below, except at the south-east corner, which is occupied by the lower part of the Chapel of St John the Evangelist.

The Chapel of St John the Evangelist is one of the most important church interiors of its date in England. Its superb simplicity, relieved only by carving to the capitals and bases, is much admired, but originally it may have been brightly coloured. The Chapel is unique among keep chapels in having aisles and a continuous tribune gallery above them.

*During the reign of Henry III (1216-72) the Chapel of St John the Evangelist was whitewashed and furnished with three stained glass windows depicting the Virgin and Child, the Holy Trinity and St John the Evangelist. Most of the existing stained glass in the Chapel was purchased in the 19th century from Horace Walpole's collection at Strawberry Hill.*

In practice, the Chapel was routinely used to store state documents, though by tradition it was the scene of some of the great events in British royal history. In 1503 the body of Elizabeth of York, wife of Henry VII, lay in state in the Chapel after her death in the Tower during childbirth. It was also here that Henry VIII's eldest daughter, Mary, was betrothed to Philip of Spain by proxy in 1554.

It is thought that this more magnificent floor was used by the king himself. The larger room may have functioned as a 'great hall', used for public gatherings, ceremonial and formal meals, the smaller one as a more private chamber. By at least the mid-12th century, however, these apartments had been duplicated by new buildings put up in the area to the south of the White Tower which gradually replaced the White Tower as royal accommodation.

*The Welsh prince Gruffudd ap Llywelyn was imprisoned in the White Tower by Henry III but fell to his death in 1244 trying to escape.*

## The Second Floor

The top floor of the building contains two main rooms, as below, and the upper part of the Chapel. Here there are the same number of windows, but a passage inside the wall thickness runs round all four sides except where interrupted by the Chapel, at which point it continues as the tribune gallery.

It is generally accepted that the rooms at this level did not exist when the White Tower was first built, and that those below rose up through it, creating two immensely high interiors overlooked by the existing gallery. This would certainly explain why there are no garderobes (lavatories) or fireplaces on this floor.

Traces of a pitched roof over each room have recently been identified on the inner faces of the north and south walls at this level. This suggests that the galleried walls here may originally have formed an external 'screen' around the top of the building, before the roof was replaced at or near its present level. Alternatively, the raising of the roof and the building of the galleried wall may have taken place at the same time – an event that the design of the wall would place before about 1100.

The second floor now houses a display about the Office of Ordnance at the Tower and a space for temporary exhibitions.

The main stair continues from the second floor to the turret above, while smaller stairs lead to the turrets over the west-facing corners.

*This engraving, dated 1805, shows the Chapel of St John the Evangelist in use as a storehouse for state records.*

In later centuries, the White Tower was put to a variety of uses. Its residential functions may have continued in some form until about 1600, even if just for prisoners; the captured French King Jean le Bon (1350-64) was lodged here in 1360, and a famous miniature shows Charles Duke of Orleans (a close relative of the French King), sitting in the White Tower in the 15th century. Its occasional use for state events continued through the Middle Ages and into the reign of Henry VIII, when it was refurbished for the coronation of Anne Boleyn in 1533. But thereafter it came to be used largely for storage, although for a few months in 1675 Charles II's 'astronomical observator', John Flamsteed, made use of the north-east turret before he moved to his new observatory at Greenwich.

The first reference to the Armouries in the White Tower dates from 1565. At first these were open at least to privileged visitors, and as early as 1599 we hear of a servant appointed to take entrance fees. But soon the building became a magazine and arms store, as well as a repository for the state papers held by the Record Office, which were kept close to the gunpowder stores. It was only in the late 19th century that most of the White Tower was open to the public, and the Armouries there became a series of displays instead of a working arsenal. This tradition lives on through the work of the Royal Armouries. The process of displaying the collection now continues beyond the walls of the Tower (at Fort Nelson near Portsmouth and at Clarence Dock, Leeds), but a wealth of material inextricably linked to the history and development of the Tower of London remains within the White Tower.

*Charles, Duke of Orleans (lived 1391-1465), imprisoned in the White Tower. This illustration is from a manuscript edition of Orleans' poetry, dating from the early 1480s, which was presented to Henry VII. It is the first detailed representation of the Tower of London.*

# THE FUSILIERS' MUSEUM

*The Museum of the Royal Regiment of Fusiliers is on the east side of the Inner Ward. Close by are two former Ordnance buildings, the Hospital Block and the New Armouries.*

*The Hospital Block was severely damaged during an air raid in 1940 and the northern part was subsequently pulled down and rebuilt.*

The Royal Regiment of Fusiliers was founded in 1685 by James II (1685-8) to protect the royal guns kept within the Tower. Two of these guns can be seen flanking the steps to the Museum. The Fusiliers were the first regiment to be armed with an improved musket, a fusil, which gave them their name.

The museum contains accounts and exhibits from the many campaigns the Regiment has been involved in, including the American War of Independence, the Napoleonic Wars, the Crimean War, the Boer War, the First and Second World Wars, the Troubles in Northern Ireland and the Gulf War. One of the more unusual exhibits is a copy of a large metal boot used in 1808 to 'cure' a malingerer by preventing him from using a corrosive substance on his leg which had kept a sore open for three and a half years. Once the boot had been applied the sore healed within twelve days!

*The New Armouries. For almost 150 years the New Armouries housed the Line of Kings, an elaborate display of mounted wooden figures representing the kings of England in their armour. The display was opened to the public in the late 17th century and survived until the 19th century.*

## The Hospital Block

The houses next to the Fusiliers' Museum were built in the early 18th century. Originally they were occupied by officials of the Board of Ordnance. Later they became the Hospital Block for the Tower garrison. Today they are the homes of Tower of London officials and are not open to the public.

## The New Armouries

This large and elegant brick building was built in 1663-4 for the Board of Ordnance as a new store for military equipment and supplies. In the 17th and 18th centuries it was only one of many stores, but it was the earliest, and today is the only one to survive. It now houses the Tower of London restaurant.

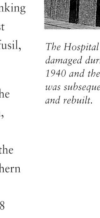

The Fusiliers' first Colonel was George Legge, Lord Dartmouth, who was also Constable of the Tower. In 1691 he was accused of conspiring against the new king, William III, and was imprisoned in the Tower where he died before he could be brought to trial.

*Main picture opposite: The Fusiliers' Museum. Built as the Officers' Mess in the mid-19th century, this building is of the same period and style as the Waterloo Barracks next to it, which was built to accommodate nearly 1,000 soldiers. Today, as well as housing the museum, the building is the Headquarters of the Royal Regiment of Fusiliers.*

# THE WHARF
## & *Tower Hill*

*These areas are outside the walls of the Tower of London and can be visited before entering or as you leave.*

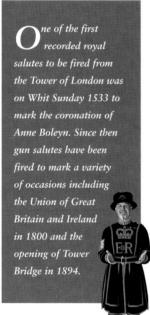

## The Wharf

When the Tower of London held the country's chief storehouse of armaments, much of the Wharf was taken up with the movement and storage of munitions, and it accommodated at different times cannon-foundries, a small arms factory and a proof yard. The Wharf also had a ceremonial role as the landing-place of royalty and of foreign dignitaries before they entered the city and since the time of Henry VIII (1509-47) guns have been fired from the Wharf on occasions of national rejoicing.

Today, royal salutes are fired from the gunpark, at the western end of the Wharf, near the Tower Shop. Four guns are brought in by a detachment of the Honourable Artillery Company, towed behind Land Rovers. Sixty-two gun salutes are fired for royal occasions: on the birthdays of The Queen (actual and official) and Prince Philip, and on the anniversary of The Queen's accession to the throne. Forty-one guns are fired at the State Opening of Parliament and when a foreign Head of State arrives on an official visit to The Queen.

*Top right: The firing of a royal salute by the Honourable Artillery Company from the gunpark on Tower Wharf.*

*Main picture opposite: The Arrival of Venetian Ambassadors at the Tower Stairs, May 1707, (detail) by the Venetian painter Luca Carlevaris (1663-1730).*

# Tower Hill

*The ramp at the top of Tower Hill takes you to Tower Hill Underground station, past the remains of the medieval city gate (on the edge of the moat). Beyond the station you can visit the site of the scaffold in Trinity Gardens.*

*Local choirboys beating the bounds of the Tower liberties with willow wands. The ceremony dates back to at least 1381 when official inspections were made of the markers. It is said that in former times the boys themselves were placed over the markers and whacked with the wands to impress the location upon them.*

Most of Tower Hill was once part of the Tower Liberty, that is the area outside the walls that was under the jurisdiction of the Tower and independent of the City of London. Its boundary is now marked by 31 boundary-stones from Tower Pier around the hill and down by St Katherine's Way to the Iron Gate Stairs near Tower Bridge. Each stone bears the broad arrow denoting royal ownership. You can see one by the entrance to Tower Pier outside the main gates of the Tower. Every third year, on Ascension Day, the Tower's authority is re-asserted in the ceremony of Beating the Bounds.

A ramp leads down to the outer curtain wall built during Edward I's expansion of the Tower between 1275 and 1285. This was originally a low parapeted wall on the edge of the new moat but soon after was raised to approximately its present height. It was still low enough, however, for defenders on the inner walls and towers to shoot across the moat and command the outer wall should it fall to the enemy.

At the north-west and north-east corners of the outer curtain wall were rounded bastions from which archers could cover the moat as well as the high ground of Tower Hill. In 1683 the bastions were reinforced and re-armed with guns. Their present names of Legge's Mount and Brass Mount date from this period.

In 1848 at the time of the Chartist riots, a third artillery bastion was built between Legge's Mount and Brass Mount to reinforce the Tower against the mob. It was destroyed by a bomb during the Second World War.

*This view of the Tower of London by George Bryant Campion (1796-1870) was made in c1840 before fire destroyed the Grand Storehouse in 1841 (its turret can be seen to the left of the White Tower) and the draining of the moat in 1843. In the foreground is Legge's Mount.*

*The Beheading of the Rebel Lords on Tower Hill, 1746. When the Earl of Kilmarnock and Lord Balmerino were executed for their part in the 1745 Jacobite Rebellion, a troop of lifeguards and 1,000 footguards were stationed around the scaffold to hold back the vast crowds of spectators.*

As you reach the subway, leading to the Underground station, you can see the excavated remains of a medieval gate, known as the Tower Hill Postern. Built soon after the completion of Edward I's new moat, around 1300, the postern was a subsidiary entrance into London through the city wall, a section of which you can see on the other side of the subway.

*The execution of a traitor from a French 15th-century manuscript. The block on display in the White Tower was made for the last beheading on Tower Hill in 1747; the axe is from the Tudor period.*

As you come up the stairs from the subway and walk past the Underground station you will see Trinity Gardens ahead of you. On the right, beyond the white memorial, lies the marked site of the scaffold on Tower Hill where some 125 Tower prisoners died, most by beheading, which was the honourable form of execution allowed to nobles and gentlemen found guilty of treason. Their deaths were watched by unruly crowds, numbering many thousands. Viewing stands were put up around the scaffold, and sometimes collapsed under the weight of eager spectators.

*The last beheading to take place in Britain was that of Simon Fraser, Lord Lovat, the last of the rebel Scottish lords to be executed after the 1745 rebellion. He was executed on Tower Hill in 1747 at the age of 80.*

Traitors of lowlier status suffered death by hanging, drawing and quartering, sometimes on the hill but most often at Tyburn (near the site of Marble Arch). Not all who died on Tower Hill were convicted traitors. Some were burned as heretics, and others hanged as common criminals, as were the last of those to be executed on this spot in 1780.

# THE HISTORY OF
## *the Tower of London*

*This penny coin was minted during the reign of William the Conqueror (1066-87) and bears a likeness of the King. After his death, an obituary of the King declared: 'he had castles built And poor men hard oppressed'.*

*This short history of the Tower of London charts the different stages of its construction and explains its role as fortress, palace and prison. The development plans on pages 4 and 5 will help you understand the evolution of the site.*

### The Normans

Castle building was an essential part of the Norman Conquest: when Duke William of Normandy invaded England in 1066 his first action after landing at Pevensey on 28 September had been to improvise a castle, and when he moved to Hastings two days later he built another. Over the next few years William and his supporters were engaged in building hundreds more, first to conquer, then subdue and finally to colonise the whole of England.

By the end of the Anglo-Saxon period London had become the most powerful city in England, with a rich port, a nearby royal palace and an important cathedral. It was via London that King Harold II (1066) and his army sped south to meet William, and to London which the defeated rabble of the English army returned from the Battle of Hastings in 1066. Securing the city was, therefore, of the utmost importance to William. His contemporary biographer William of Poitiers tells us that after receiving the submission of the English magnates at Little Berkhampstead, William sent an advance guard into London to construct a castle and prepare for his triumphal entry. He also tells us that, after his coronation in Westminster Abbey on Christmas Day 1066, the new King withdrew to Barking (in Essex)

'while certain fortifications were completed in the city against the restlessness of the vast and fierce populace for he realised that it was of the first importance to overawe the Londoners'.

These fortifications may have included Baynard's Castle built in the south-west angle of the city (near Blackfriars) and the castle of Monfichet (near Ludgate Circus) and almost certainly the future Tower

*A 14th-century manuscript illumination showing William the Conqueror and his Norman army defeating King Harold II at the Battle of Hastings in 1066.*

*Main picture opposite: The Tower of London from the west by Johannes Spilberg, c1689 (detail).*

*William the Conqueror, depicted on the Bayeux Tapestry. The Bayeux Tapestry provides a unique pictorial representation of the principal events of the Norman Conquest of England in 1066.*

of London. Initially the Tower had consisted of a modest enclosure built into the south-east corner of the Roman city walls, but by the late 1070s, with the initial completion of the White Tower, it had become the most fearsome of all. Nothing had been seen like it in England before. It was built by Norman masons and English (Anglo-Saxon) labour drafted in from the countryside, perhaps to the design of Gundulf, Bishop of Rochester. It was intended to protect the river route from Danish attack, but also and more importantly to dominate the city physically and visually. It is difficult to appreciate today what an enormous impression the Tower and other Norman buildings, such as St Paul's Cathedral (as rebuilt after 1086) or the nearby Westminster Hall (rebuilt after 1087) must have made on the native Londoners.

The White Tower was protected to the east and south by the old Roman city walls (a full height fragment can be seen just by Tower Hill Underground station), while the north and west sides were protected by ditches as much as 7.50m (25ft) wide and 3.40m (11ft) deep and an earthwork with a wooden wall on top. In the 12th century a 'fore-building' (now demolished) was added to the south front of the White Tower to protect the entrance. The Wardrobe Tower, a fragment of which can be seen at the south-east corner of the building, was another early addition or rebuilding. From very early on the enclosure contained a number of timber buildings for residential and service use. It is not clear whether these included a royal residence but William the Conqueror's immediate successors probably made use of the White Tower itself.

It is important for us today to remember that the functions of the Tower from the 1070s until the late 19th century were established by its Norman founders. The Tower was never primarily intended to protect London from external invasion, although, of course, it could have done so if necessary. Nor was it ever intended to be the principal residence of the kings and queens of England, though many did in fact spend periods of time there. Its primary function was always to provide a base for royal power in the City of London and a stronghold to which the royal family could retreat in times of civil disorder.

## The Medieval Tower:
### A Refuge and a Base for Royal Power

When Richard the Lionheart (1189-99) came to the
throne he departed on a crusade to the Holy Land
leaving his Chancellor, William Longchamp, Bishop
of Ely, in charge of the kingdom. Longchamp soon
embarked on an enlargement and strengthening
of the Tower of London, the first of a series of
building campaigns which by about 1350 had
created the basic form of the great fortress that we know today. The
justification for the vast expenditure and effort this involved was the
political instability of the kingdom and the Crown's continuing need for
an impregnable fortress in the City of London.

Longchamp's works doubled the area covered by the fortress by digging
a new and deeper ditch to the north and east and building sections of
curtain wall, reinforced by a new tower (now known as the Bell Tower)
at the south-west corner. The ditch was intended to flood naturally
from the river, although this was not a success. These new defences were
soon put to the test when the King's brother, John, taking advantage of
Richard's absence, challenged Longchamp's authority and besieged him
at the Tower. Lack of provisions forced Longchamp to surrender but the
Tower's defences had proved that they could resist attack.

The reign of the next king, John (1199-1216), saw little new
building work at the Tower, but the King made good use of
the accommodation there. Like Longchamp, John had to
cope with frequent opposition throughout his reign. Only a
year after signing an agreement with his barons in 1215 (the
Magna Carta) they were once more at loggerheads and Prince
Louis of France had launched an invasion of England with
the support of some of John's leading barons. In the midst of
his defence of the kingdom, John died of dysentery and his
son, Henry III, was crowned.

*King John made good use of
the royal accommodation at
the Tower of London and
between 1203 and his death
in 1216 made 28 visits, staying
for over ten weeks. This
14th-century manuscript
illumination shows the King
hunting.*

With England at war with France, the start of King Henry's
long reign (1216-72) could have hardly been less auspicious,
but within seven months of his accession the French had been
defeated at the battle of Lincoln and the business of securing
the kingdom could begin. Reinforcement of the royal castles
played a major role in this, and his work at the Tower of London was
more extensive than anywhere other than at Windsor Castle. Henry III
was only 10 years old in 1216, but his regents began a major extension
of the royal accommodation in the enclosure that formed the Inmost
Ward as we know it today. The great hall and kitchen, dating from the
previous century, were improved and two towers built on the waterfront,
the Wakefield Tower as the King's lodgings and the Lanthorn Tower
(rebuilt in the 19th century), probably intended as the queen's lodgings.
A new wall was also built enclosing the west side of the Inmost Ward.

*During the long reign of
Henry III (1216-72) hardly a
year went by when work was
not in progress somewhere
within the walls of the Tower.
This contemporary illustration
shows the coronation of
the King.*

47

*A late 15th-century depiction of Joan of Arc's siege of Paris in 1429. It shows defences similar to the 13th and 14th-century outer walls of the Tower of London in active use; note in particular the twin-towered gatehouse, complete with drawbridge (not unlike the Byward or Middle towers) and the crenellated curtain wall lapped by a water-filled moat (as existed at the Tower until 1843).*

By the mid-1230s, Henry III had run into trouble with his barons and opposition flared up in both 1236 and in 1238. On both occasions the King fled to the Tower of London. But as he sheltered in the castle in March 1238 the weakness of the Tower must have been brought home to him; the defences to the eastern, western and northern sides consisted only of an empty moat, stretches of patched-up and strengthened Roman wall and a few lengths of wall built by Longchamp in the previous century. That year, therefore, saw the launch of Henry's most ambitious building programme at the Tower, the construction of a great new curtain wall round the east, north and west sides of the castle at a cost of over £5,000 (in modern terms about £1.8 million). The new wall doubled the area covered by the fortress, enclosing the neighbouring church of St Peter ad Vincula. It was surrounded by a moat, this time successfully flooded by a Flemish engineer, John Le Fosser. The wall was reinforced by nine new towers, the strongest at the corners (the Salt, Martin and Devereux). Of these all but two (the Flint and Brick) are much as originally built. This massive extension to the Tower was viewed with extreme suspicion and hostility by the people of London, who rightly recognised it as a further assertion of royal authority. A contemporary writer reports their delight when a section of newly built wall and a gateway on the site of the Beauchamp Tower collapsed, events they attributed to their own guardian saint, Thomas à Becket. Archaeological excavation between 1995 and 1997 revealed the remains of one of these collapsed buildings.

*Edward I continued his father's expansion of the Tower and by the end of his reign it had become one of the greatest castles in the land. This illustration shows the King investing his son Edward (later Edward II) as the first Prince of Wales in February 1301.*

In 1272 King Edward I (1272-1307) came to the throne determined to complete and extend the defensive works begun by his father. Between 1275 and 1285 the King spent over £21,000 (about £7.6 million in modern money) on the fortress creating England's largest and strongest concentric castle (a castle with one line of defences within another). The work included building the existing Beauchamp Tower, but the main effort was concentrated on filling in Henry III's moat and creating an additional curtain wall on all four sides, and surrounding it by a new moat. This wall enclosed the existing curtain wall built by Henry III and was pierced by two new entrances, one from the land on the west, passing through the Middle and Byward towers, and another under St Thomas's Tower, from the river. New royal lodgings were included in the upper part of St Thomas's Tower. Almost all these buildings survive in some form today.

Despite all this work Edward was a very rare visitor to his fortress; he was, in fact, only able to enjoy his new lodgings there for a few days. There is no doubt though that if he had been a weaker king, and had had to put up with disorders in London of the kind experienced by his father and grandfather, the Tower would have come into its own as an even more effective and efficient base for royal authority.

King Edward's new works were, however, put to the test by his son, Edward II (1307-27), whose reign saw a resurgence of discontent among the

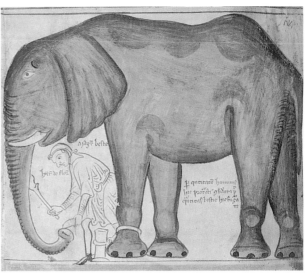

barons on a scale not seen since the reign of his grandfather. Once again the Tower played a crucial role in the attempt to maintain royal authority and as a royal refuge. Edward II did little more than improve the walls put up by his father, but he was a regular resident during his turbulent reign and he moved his own lodgings from the Wakefield Tower and St Thomas's Tower to the area round the present Lanthorn Tower. The old royal lodgings were now used for his courtiers and for the storage of official papers by the King's Wardrobe (a department of government which dealt with royal supplies). The use of the Tower for functions other than military and residential had been started by Edward I who put up a large new building to house the Royal Mint and began to use the castle as a place for storing records. As early as the reign of Henry III the castle had already been in regular use as a prison: Hubert de Burgh, Chief Justiciar of England was incarcerated in 1232 and the Welsh Prince Gruffudd was imprisoned there between 1241 and 1244, when he fell to his death in a bid to escape. The Tower also served as a treasury (the Crown Jewels were moved from Westminster Abbey to the Tower in 1303) and as a showplace for the king's animals.

*The Tower was first used as a menagerie in the reign of Henry III. The King's collection of animals included an elephant presented by King Louis of France in 1255, and said to be the first seen in England. It was kept at the Tower in a specially-built elephant house.*

After the unstable reign of Edward II came that of Edward III (1327-77). Edward III's works at the Tower were fairly minor, but he did put up a new gatehouse between the Lanthorn Tower and the Salt Tower, together with the Cradle Tower and its postern (a small subsidiary entrance), a further postern behind the Byward Tower and another at the Develin Tower. He was also responsible for rebuilding the upper parts of the Bloody Tower and creating the vault over the gate passage, but his most substantial achievement was to extend the Tower Wharf eastwards as far as St Thomas's Tower. This was completed in its present form by his successor Richard II (1377-99).

*Edward III was one of England's greatest royal builders and he spent much time at the Tower, enjoying it as a residence rather than using it as a refuge. Here he is seen with his eldest son Edward, the 'Black Prince'.*

*Richard II's reign saw the introduction of a tradition that remained associated with the Tower until the reign of Charles II – it became the starting point for the great coronation day procession through the streets of London to Westminster Abbey.*

Richard II's reign brought to an end the peaceful interlude under Edward III. During the Peasants' Revolt of 1381 the 14-year-old King and many of his family and household were forced to shelter in the Tower while over 10,000 rebels plundered and burnt the capital for two days. The King and his queen sheltered there again in 1387, when the barons clashed with the King's favourite, Robert de Vere, Earl of Oxford. Just as Richard's reign had begun at the Tower of London, so did it end: on 1 October 1399 the King, condemned as a tyrant, renounced the crown in his chamber in the White Tower and Henry IV was proclaimed King the next day.

The reigns of Henry IV (1399-1413) and Henry V (1413-22) were quiet ones for the Tower of London; no great new building works were undertaken, nor was the fortress at the centre of great political or military events.

During the reign of Henry VI (1422-61 and 1470-1) England entered the period of civil disorder and political instability known as the Wars of the Roses. Throughout this period the Tower of London was a key asset to those who held the throne or wished to.

In victory Edward IV (1461-70 and 1471-83) held lavish courts there in 1465 and 1470; Richard III (1483-5) presided over splendid celebrations for his coronation in 1483 and finally Henry VII (1485-1509) entertained his victorious supporters there after he had won the throne in 1485. For the defeated and helpless, on the other hand, the Tower was the scene of murder and execution; victims included Henry VI himself in 1471, the young Edward V and his brother (the 'Princes in the Tower') in 1483, and George, Duke of Clarence in 1478 (allegedly drowned in a butt of wine).

During this period the Tower's defences were vigorously maintained and minor improvements made, notably in about 1480 when Edward IV built a new brick bulwark (outer defence) beyond the western entrance.

*During the Peasants' Revolt (against the introduction of a crown or royal poll tax) the Tower of London was besieged by a crowd of rebels who murdered several members of the King's household and looted the armoury and Jewel House. This scene shows the death of one of the rebel leaders, Wat Tyler, in front of the 14-year-old Richard II.*

## The Tower in Tudor Times:

### *A Royal Prison*

The first Tudor monarch, Henry VII (1485-1509) was responsible for building the last permanent royal residential buildings at the Tower. He extended his own lodgings around the Lanthorn Tower adding a new private chamber, a library, a long gallery, and also laid out a garden. These buildings were to form the nucleus of a much larger scheme begun by his son Henry VIII (1509-47) who put up a large range of timber-framed lodgings at the time of the coronation of his second wife, Anne Boleyn. The building of these lodgings, used only once, marked the end of the history of royal residence at the Tower.

*When Henry VIII became king in 1509 he had the Tower completely re-stocked with new armour and weapons.*

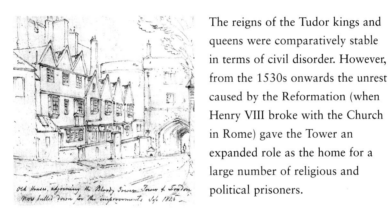

*This 19th-century drawing by T.H. Shepherd shows the row of timber-framed buildings erected by Henry VIII in 1533 against the wall of the Inmost Ward. They were only demolished in 1846.*

The reigns of the Tudor kings and queens were comparatively stable in terms of civil disorder. However, from the 1530s onwards the unrest caused by the Reformation (when Henry VIII broke with the Church in Rome) gave the Tower an expanded role as the home for a large number of religious and political prisoners.

The first important Tudor prisoners were Sir Thomas More and Bishop Fisher of Rochester, both of whom were executed in 1535 for refusing to acknowledge Henry VIII as head of the English Church. They were soon followed by a still more famous prisoner and victim, the King's second wife, Anne Boleyn, executed along with her brother and four others a little under a year later. July 1540 saw the execution of Thomas Cromwell, Earl of Essex and former chief minister of the King – in which capacity he had modernised the Tower's defences and, ironically enough, sent many others to their deaths on the same spot. Two years later, Catherine Howard, the second of Henry VIII's six wives to be beheaded, met her death outside the Chapel of St Peter ad Vincula that Henry had rebuilt a few years before.

*Bishop Fisher of Rochester – executed on Tower Hill in 1535.*

*Thomas Cromwell – executed on Tower Hill in 1540.*

The reign of Edward VI (1547-53) saw a continuation of the political executions which had begun in his father's reign; the young King's protector, the Duke of Somerset, and his confederates met their death at the Tower in 1552, falsely accused of treason. During Edward's reign the English Church became more Protestant, but the King's early death in 1553 left the country with a Catholic heir, Mary I (1553-8). During

*Edward Seymour, Duke of Somerset – executed on Tower Hill in 1552.*

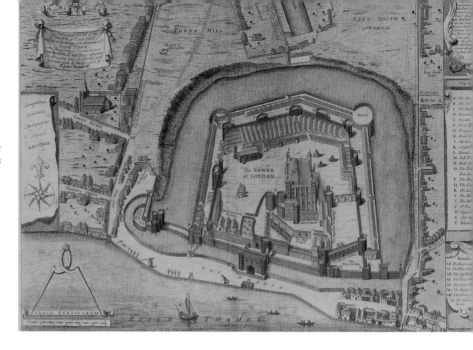

*Mary I – ordered the
imprisonment and execution
of many religious and
political opponents.*

*Princess Elizabeth (later
Elizabeth I) – imprisoned in
the Tower in 1554.*

her brief reign many important Protestants and political rivals were
either imprisoned or executed at the Tower. The most famous victim was
Lady Jane Grey, and the most famous prisoner the Queen's half-sister
Princess Elizabeth (the future Elizabeth I). Religious controversy did not
end with Mary's death in 1558; Queen Elizabeth I (1558-1603) spent
much of her reign warding off the threat from Catholic Europe, and
important recusants (people who refused to attend Church of England
services) and others who might have opposed her rule were locked up in
the Tower. Never had it been so full of prisoners, or such illustrious ones:
bishops, archbishops, knights, barons, earls and dukes all spent months
and some of them years languishing in the towers of the Tower of
London.

Little was done to the Tower's defences in these years. The Royal Mint
was modified and extended, new storehouses were built for royal military
supplies. In the reign of James I (1603-25) the Lieutenant's house – built
in the 1540s and today called the Queen's House – was extended and
modified; the king's lions were rehoused in better dens made for them in
the west gate barbican (the Lion Tower).

## The Restoration and After:
### The Tower and the Office of Ordnance

After a long period of peace at home, the reign of Charles I (1625-49)
saw civil war break out again in 1642, between King and Parliament.
As during the Wars of the Roses and previous conflicts, the Tower was
recognised as one of the most important of the King's assets. Londoners,
in particular, were frightened that the Tower would be used by him to
dominate the city. In 1643, after a political rather than a military struggle,
control of the Tower was seized from the King by the parliamentarians
and remained in their hands throughout the Civil War (1642-9). The
loss of the Tower, and of London as a whole, was a crucial factor in
the defeat of Charles I by Parliament. It was during this period that a
permanent garrison was installed in the Tower for the first time, by
Oliver Cromwell, soon to be Lord Protector but then a prominent
parliamentary commander. Today's small military guard, seen outside the

Queen's House and the Waterloo Barracks, is an echo of Cromwell's innovation.

The monarchy was restored in 1660 and the reign of the new king, Charles II (1660-85), saw further changes in the functions of the Tower. Its role as a state prison declined and the Office of Ordnance (which provided military supplies and equipment) took over responsibility for most of the castle, making it their headquarters. During this period another long-standing tradition of the Tower began – the public display of the Crown Jewels. They were moved from their old home to a new site in what is now called the Martin Tower, and put on show by their keeper Talbot Edwards.

*The Tower of London by W. Hollar, c1660. Following the restoration of the monarchy in 1660, Charles II ordered major improvements to the Tower's defences. A large permanent garrison was housed in the Tower, batteries of guns were set in place along the walls and the arsenal was expanded.*

Schemes for strengthening the Tower's defences, some elaborate and up to date, were also proposed so that in the event of violent opposition, which was always a possibility during the 1660s and 1670s, Charles would not be caught out as his father had been earlier in the century. In the end, none of these came to much, and the Restoration period saw only a minor strengthening of the Tower. Yet the well-equipped garrison that Charles II and his successors maintained was often used to quell disturbances in the city; James II (1685-8) certainly took steps to use the Tower's forces against the opposition which eventually caused him to flee into exile.

Under the control of the Office of Ordnance, the Tower was filled with a series of munitions stores and workshops for the army and navy. The most impressive and elegant of these was the Grand Storehouse begun in 1688 on the site where the Waterloo Barracks now stand. It was initially a weapons store but as the 17th century drew to a close it became more of a museum of arms and armour. More utilitarian buildings gradually took over the entire area previously covered by the medieval royal lodgings to the south of the White Tower; by 1800, after a series of fires and rebuildings, the whole of this area had become a mass of large brick Ordnance buildings. All these, however, have been swept away, and the only surviving storehouse put up by the Ordnance is the New Armouries, standing against the eastern inner curtain wall between the Salt and Broad Arrow towers.

*The late 18th-century Ordnance Office from the east end of the Wharf, seen here in 1882 shortly before the building was demolished.*

While the Ordnance was busy building storehouses, offices and workshops, the army was expanding accommodation for the Tower garrison. Their largest building was the Irish Barracks (now demolished), sited behind the New Armouries building in the Outer Ward.

## The Tower in the 19th Century:
*From Fortress to Ancient Monument*

Between 1800 and 1900 the Tower of London took on the appearance that to a large extent it retains today. Early in the century many of the historic institutions that had been based within its walls began to move out. The first to go was the Mint, which moved to new buildings to the north east of the castle in 1812, where it remained until 1968, when it moved to its present location near Cardiff. The Royal Menagerie left the Lion Tower in 1834 to become the nucleus of what is now London Zoo, and the Record Office (responsible for storing documents of state), moved to Chancery Lane during the 1850s, vacating parts of the medieval royal lodgings and the White Tower. Finally, after the War Office assumed responsibility for the manufacture and storage of weapons in 1855, large areas of the fortress were vacated by the old Office of Ordnance.

*In October 1841 a great fire at the Tower of London completely destroyed the Grand Storehouse and its vast collection of weapons.*

However, before these changes took place the Tower had once again – but for the last time – performed its traditional role in asserting the authority of the state over the people of London. The Chartist movement of the 1840s (which sought major political reform) prompted a final refortification of the Tower between 1848 and 1852, and further work was carried out in 1862. To protect the approaches to the Tower new loop-holes and gun emplacements were built and an enormous brick and stone bastion (destroyed by a bomb during the Second World War) constructed on the north side of the fortress. Following the burning down of the Grand Storehouse in 1841, the present Waterloo Barracks was put up to accommodate 1,000 soldiers, and the Brick, Flint and Bowyer towers to its north were altered or rebuilt to service it; the Royal Fusiliers' building was erected at the same time to be the officers' mess. The mob never stormed the castle but the fear of it left the outer defences of the Tower much as they are today.

*The Stone Kitchen tavern that stood to the west of the Bell Tower. This drawing by T.H. Shepherd was made shortly before the building was pulled down in 1846.*

The vacation of large parts of the Tower by the offices that had formerly occupied it and an increasing interest in the history and archaeology of the Tower led, after 1850, to a programme of 're-medievalisation'. By then the late 17th and 18th-century Ordnance buildings and barracks, together with a series of private inns and taverns, such as the Stone Kitchen and the Golden Chain, had obscured most of the medieval fortress. The first clearances of these buildings began in the late 1840s, but the real work began in 1852, when the architect Anthony Salvin, already known for his work on medieval buildings, re-exposed the Beauchamp Tower and restored it to a medieval appearance. Salvin's work was much admired and attracted the attention of Prince Albert (husband of Queen Victoria), who recommended that he be made responsible for a complete restoration

of the castle. This led to a programme of work which involved the Salt Tower, the White Tower, St Thomas's Tower, the Bloody Tower and the construction of two new houses on Tower Green (numbers 7 and 8).

In the 1870s Salvin was replaced by John Taylor, a less talented and sensitive architect. His efforts concentrated on the southern parts of the Tower, notably the Cradle and Develin towers and on the demolition of the 18th-century Ordnance Office and storehouse on the site of the Lanthorn Tower, which he rebuilt. He also built the stretches of wall linking the Lanthorn Tower to the Salt and Wakefield towers. But by the 1890s, restoration of this type was going out of fashion and this was the last piece of re-medievalisation to be undertaken. The work of this period had succeeded in opening up the site and re-exposing its defences, but fell far short of restoring its true medieval appearance.

*This watercolour by John Crowther, dated 1883, shows the demolition of the Horse Armoury against the south face of the White Tower and in the foreground, the site of the late 18th-century Ordnance Office where the Lanthorn Tower was later rebuilt.*

The second half of the 19th century saw a great increase in the number of visitors to the Tower, although sightseers had been admitted as early as 1660. In 1841 the first official guidebook was issued and ten years later a purpose-built ticket office was erected at the western entrance. By the end of Queen Victoria's reign in 1901, half a million people were visiting the Tower each year.

## The 20th Century

The First World War (1914-18) left the Tower largely untouched; the only bomb to fall on the fortress landed in the moat. However, the war brought the Tower of London back into use as a prison for the first time since the early 19th century and between 1914 and 1916 eleven spies were held and subsequently executed in the Tower. The last execution in the Tower took place in 1941 during the Second World War (1939-45). Bomb damage to the Tower during the Second World War was much greater: a number of buildings were severely damaged or destroyed including the mid-19th-century North Bastion, which received a direct hit on 5 October 1940, and the Hospital Block which was partly destroyed during an air raid in the same year. Incendiaries also destroyed the Main Guard, a late 19th-century building to the south west of the White Tower.

*Vegetable allotments in the moat during the Second World War.*

During the Second World War the Tower was closed to the public. The moat, which had been drained and filled in 1843, was used as allotments for vegetable growing and the Crown Jewels were removed from the Tower and taken to a place of safety, the location of which has never been disclosed.

Today the Tower of London is one of the world's major tourist attractions and over 2 million visitors a year come from all corners of the world to discover its long and eventful history, its buildings, ceremonies and traditions.

# THE COMMUNITY
## of the Tower

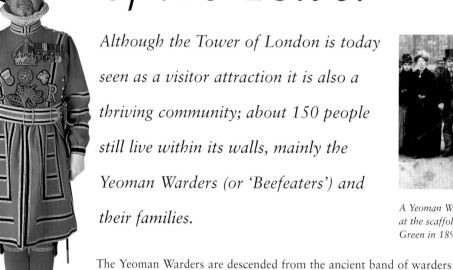

*Although the Tower of London is today seen as a visitor attraction it is also a thriving community; about 150 people still live within its walls, mainly the Yeoman Warders (or 'Beefeaters') and their families.*

*A Yeoman Warder with visitors at the scaffold site on Tower Green in 1895.*

The Yeoman Warders are descended from the ancient band of warders who, from early in the Tower's history, had the responsibility for guarding the gates and royal prisoners. From the reign of Henry VIII (1509-47), these duties were carried out by the King's Yeomen at the Tower who were entitled to wear the royal livery – a version of which is still worn. The uniform which most visitors see today is the blue undress uniform introduced in 1858 and worn as the Yeoman Warders' normal working dress. The red and gold state dress is only worn for special occasions, ceremonies, church parades and when royalty visits the Tower. Modern Yeoman Warders (of whom there are about 35) are still Extraordinary Members of The Queen's Bodyguard and are all former warrant officers from Her Majesty's Forces with an honourable service record of at least 22 years.

*The Chief Yeoman Warder with his mace of office.*

As well as the Yeoman Warders, the Tower is guarded by a military guard detailed for duty from the same regiments that guard Buckingham Palace and St James's Palace. They join the Yeoman Warders each night for the ancient Ceremony of the Keys (open to the public by application in advance). At this ceremony, a version of which has been performed nightly for hundreds of years, the outer gates of the fortress are locked and the keys delivered to the Resident Governor of the Tower.

*The conclusion of the Ceremony of the Keys. The Chief Yeoman Warder raises his hat and calls 'God preserve Queen Elizabeth' and the guard and escort respond 'Amen'. Then the Last Post echoes round Tower Green.*

Since its earliest days, there has always been someone in local command of the Tower. Originally this was the Constable, an office dating from the 11th century when William the Conqueror appointed Geoffrey de Mandeville as his representative. Later, the Constable's duties were performed by a Lieutenant, then a Deputy Lieutenant and Major, and since 1858 by the Resident Governor.

The post of Constable still exists, although the daily administration of the fortress is overseen by the Resident Governor. To date there have been 158 Constables. A new Constable is appointed every five years and the installation ceremony takes place on Tower Green where the Lord Chamberlain, as the monarch's representative, hands the Constable the gold keys to the Tower as a symbol of his custodianship. The Constable then hands the keys of the Queen's House to the Resident Governor, granting him permission to live there.

As well as the Yeoman Warders, the Governor and the military guard, the Tower is home to its own Chaplain and Doctor and perhaps most famously, to the Ravens. It is not known when the Ravens first came to the Tower but their presence is protected by a legend that without them

*The Duke of Wellington was Constable of the Tower for 26 years from 1826 to his death in 1852. During his administration the Tower's military role was re-asserted and its defences strengthened. The Duke even tried to exclude the visiting public which he considered to be a threat to the Tower's security.*

*The Ravenmaster with one of the Tower Ravens.*

the Tower and the kingdom will fall. The story goes that Charles II's 'astronomical observator', John Flamsteed (1646-1719), complained to the King that the Ravens were interfering with his observations from the north-east turret of the White Tower. The King then ordered the destruction of the birds, only to be told that without them the Tower would fall and the kingdom with it. To prevent such a catastrophe, a limited number was, therefore, allowed to remain. The wings of the birds are now clipped to prevent them from flying away.

Ravens can live for about 25 years, so deaths are not common, but when one does die it is usually replaced by a wild one, although in recent years some have been hatched in captivity. The Ravens are cared for by one of the Yeoman Warders, with the title of Ravenmaster. Their lodgings are adjacent to the Wakefield Tower.

*Yeoman Warders in state dress during the reign of Queen Victoria (1837-1901).*

# KINGS & QUEENS
## *of Great Britain*

| | | | | |
|---|---|---|---|---|
| **THE NORMANS** | WILLIAM I | 1066 | *to* | 1087 |
| | WILLIAM II | 1087 | *to* | 1100 |
| | HENRY I | 1100 | *to* | 1135 |
| | STEPHEN | 1135 | *to* | 1154 |

*The coat of arms of William I*

| | | | | |
|---|---|---|---|---|
| **THE PLANTAGENETS** | HENRY II | 1154 | *to* | 1189 |
| | RICHARD I | 1189 | *to* | 1199 |
| | JOHN | 1199 | *to* | 1216 |
| | HENRY III | 1216 | *to* | 1272 |
| | EDWARD I | 1272 | *to* | 1307 |
| | EDWARD II | 1307 | *to* | 1327 |
| | EDWARD III | 1327 | *to* | 1377 |
| | RICHARD II | 1377 | *to* | 1399 |
| | HENRY IV | 1399 | *to* | 1413 |
| | HENRY V | 1413 | *to* | 1422 |
| | HENRY VI | 1422 | *to* | 1461 |
| | | 1470 | *to* | 1471 |
| | EDWARD IV | 1461 | *to* | 1470 |
| | | 1471 | *to* | 1483 |
| | EDWARD V | 1483 | | |
| | RICHARD III | 1483 | *to* | 1485 |

*A groat of Edward I*

| | | | | |
|---|---|---|---|---|
| **THE TUDORS** | HENRY VII | 1485 | *to* | 1509 |
| | HENRY VIII | 1509 | *to* | 1547 |
| | EDWARD VI | 1547 | *to* | 1553 |
| | MARY I | 1553 | *to* | 1558 |
| | ELIZABETH I | 1558 | *to* | 1603 |

| | | | | |
|---|---|---|---|---|
| **THE STUARTS** | JAMES I | 1603 | *to* | 1625 |
| | CHARLES I | 1625 | *to* | 1649 |
| | THE COMMONWEALTH | 1649 | *to* | 1660 |
| | CHARLES II | 1660 | *to* | 1685 |
| | JAMES II | 1685 | *to* | 1688 |
| | WILLIAM III | 1689 | *to* | 1702 |
| | & MARY II | 1689 | *to* | 1694 |
| | ANNE | 1702 | *to* | 1714 |

*Miniature of William III*

| | | | | |
|---|---|---|---|---|
| **THE HANOVERIANS** | GEORGE I | 1714 | *to* | 1727 |
| | GEORGE II | 1727 | *to* | 1760 |
| | GEORGE III | 1760 | *to* | 1820 |
| | GEORGE IV | 1820 | *to* | 1830 |
| | WILLIAM IV | 1830 | *to* | 1837 |
| | VICTORIA | 1837 | *to* | 1901 |

| | | | | |
|---|---|---|---|---|
| **THE HOUSE OF WINDSOR** | EDWARD VII | 1901 | *to* | 1910 |
| | GEORGE V | 1910 | *to* | 1936 |
| | EDWARD VIII | 1936 | | |
| | GEORGE VI | 1936 | *to* | 1952 |
| | ELIZABETH II | Succeeded | | 1952 |

*Miniature of Queen Victoria*

# GLOSSARY
## & Acknowledgments

| | |
|---|---|
| *Arsenal:* | An establishment for the manufacture and storage of arms and ammunition. |
| *Barbican:* | An outer defence protecting the entrance to a castle. |
| *Bastion:* | A projecting part of a fortress, especially one at the angle of a wall, from which the ground before the wall or rampart is defended. |
| *Capital:* | The head or crowning feature of a column. |
| *Castellated:* | Having battlements, or other 'military' features. |
| *Crenellation:* | Battlement or raised part of parapet, with openings to either side. |
| *Curtain wall:* | A wall enclosing a castle or one of its parts. |
| *Embrasure:* | A recess for a window, door, etc, or a small opening in a defensive wall or parapet (usually splayed on the inside) used as a shooting position. |
| *Loop:* | A narrow vertical slit in a defensive wall, from which bows and guns could be shot. The interior of the loop was often deeply splayed to increase the angle of fire. |
| *Mural towers:* | Wall towers. |
| *Neo-gothic:* | A modern form of Gothic architecture (the style prevalent in Western Europe from the 12th to the 15th century) popular in the 19th century. |
| *Portcullis:* | A heavy iron or wooden grating lowered vertically as a defensive barrier at the entrance of a gatehouse. |
| *Proof yard:* | A place for testing cannon or small fire-arms. |
| *Romanesque:* | The style of architecture current in the 11th and 12th centuries, characterised by round arches and vaults. |
| *Slits:* | See loop. |
| *Vault:* | An arched ceiling or roof, usually of stone or brick. |
| *Windlass:* | A mechanical device for raising weights by winding a rope or chain upon a barrel or drum driven by a crank. |

### Illustrations

Unless otherwise stated, all illustrations are Crown Copyright: Historic Royal Palaces.
Principal photography by Jan Baldwin and Paul Windsor. Crown Jewels photography by David Chalmers.
Additional photography by Earl Beesley: page 10b and Cliff Birtchnell page 34c.

*Abbreviations:* b = bottom; c = centre; l = left; r = right, t = top

The Marquess of Bath, Longleat House, Warminster, Wiltshire: page 51rb. Bayerische Staatsgemäldesammlungen: page 40. Bibliothèque Nationale, Paris/Bridgeman Art Library, London: page 48t. The British Library: pages 13b (Cott MS Vit. AXIII, f.6v), 14t (Cott Nero D II f.179v), 35c (Cott Aug A III f.35), 36b (Royal 14 C VII f.136), 37b (Royal MS 16 F ii f.73), 43c (Roy 20 C VII f.134v). The British Library/Bridgeman Art Library, London: pages 19t (Add 10294 f.81b), 45b (Cott Vitt A XIII f.3v), 47t (Cott Claud DII f.113), 47b (Cott Vitt A XIII f.6), 48b (Cott Nero D II f.191v), 50b (Roy 18 E I f.175). The Trustees of the British Museum: pages 16b, 53t. The Trustees of the British Museum/Bridgeman Art Library, London: page 45t. Camera Press, London: page 23t. Collections/Bartholomew: pages 34b, 41t. Collections/Brian Shuel: page 42t. The Master and Fellows of Corpus Christi College, Cambridge: page 49t (CCC MS 16 f.ivr). Musée de la Tapisserie, Bayeux/Giraudon/Bridgeman Art Library, London: page 46. © Crown Copyright: UK Government Art Collection: pages 27b, 44. Greater London Record Office: page 37t. The Guildhall Library, Corporation of London: pages 4-5 (background), 7t, 8t, 13t, 20t, 43t, 51l, 54b, 56r, 55t, 58 (background). The Guildhall Library, Corporation of London/Bridgeman Art Library, London: page 42b, 54t. Hulton Getty: page 55b. The National Library of Scotland, Edinburgh/Bridgeman Art Library, London: page 20c. The National Portrait Gallery, London: pages 10t, 28c, 30rt, 43b, 51t, 51rc, 52lt, 57t, 58r4. Private Collection/Bridgeman Art Library, London: page 49b. The Board of Trustees of the Royal Armouries: pages 7b, 15b, 23b, 35t, 53b. The Royal Collection © 1996 Her Majesty The Queen: pages 24t, 30rb, 51rt, 52lb. Royal Holloway & Bedford New College, Surrey/Bridgeman Art Library, London: page 28b. Courtesy of the Royal Mint: page 58r2. Jane Thompson, Heraldic Illustrator: page 58r1. The Trustees of the Victoria & Albert Museum: pages 10c, 21b, 58r3. Westminster Abbey, London/Bridgeman Art Library, London: page 50t.

Crown Copyright © 1996. This edition published by Historic Royal Palaces 2004.

Written by Simon Thurley, Edward Impey and Peter Hammond; edited by Clare Murphy and Anne Fletcher; picture research by Clare Murphy; designed by Schneider Associates Ltd; all foreign language editions by SR Translations (www.srtranslations.co.uk); printed by Wyndeham Westway Ltd (www.wyndeham.co.uk).

The exhibition *Crowns and Diamonds: the making of the Crown Jewels* has been made possible by the generosity of De Beers. Their contribution is gratefully acknowledged.

# Other Historic Royal Palaces to visit

## Hampton Court Palace

*The greatest palace in Britain*

Take a magical history tour through 500 years of royal history. Discover what life was like at the courts of Henry VIII and William III with costumed guides and family trails. Marvel at great works of art from the Royal Collection, stroll through 60 acres of riverside gardens or lose yourself in the famous maze. For enquiries, telephone 0870 752 7777; ticket sales 0870 753 7777.

## Kensington Palace

*The fabric of royal history*

Birthplace of Queen Victoria, Kensington was acquired by William III and Mary II in 1689 and remains a royal home today. The State Apartments are open to visitors throughout the year and include the Royal Ceremonial Dress Collection with dresses worn by Queen Elizabeth II and Diana, Princess of Wales. For enquiries, telephone 0870 751 5170; ticket sales 0870 751 5180.

## The Banqueting House, Whitehall

*The original setting for royal banquets*

The Banqueting House, with its magnificent Rubens ceiling, was designed by the renowned architect Inigo Jones in the early 17th century and is today the only remaining part of Whitehall Palace. Charles I, the only English monarch to be executed, met his fate here. For enquiries, telephone 0870 751 5178.

## Kew Palace & Queen Charlotte's Cottage

*Royal residence in the gardens*

Set in the spectacular surroundings of the Royal Botanic Gardens Kew, these two delightful buildings were used by the royal family in the 18th and early 19th century and are particularly associated with George III, Queen Charlotte and their family. **Kew Palace is currently closed for conservation and re-presentation.** For enquiries, telephone 0870 751 5179.

**Tower of London enquiries,** telephone 0870 756 6060; ticket sales 0870 756 7070.

The Tower of London is managed by Historic Royal Palaces, a Registered Charity (No. 1068852), which has a wholly owned trading subsidiary, Historic Royal Palaces Enterprises Limited, a company registered in England (No. 3418583). The registered office and address for service of both bodies is Hampton Court Palace, Surrey, KT8 9AU.

Historic Royal Palaces is responsible for the care, conservation and presentation of some of Britain's most important historic buildings and their collections. We receive no public funding and rely on visitor income and donations to fund the vital conservation and education work that we undertake. Please help us to preserve these unique landmarks for future generations. If you would like to make a donation, please email www.development@hrp.org.uk or telephone 020 8781 9786 for further information.

Visit our Web site: **www.hrp.org.uk** for more information on the Historic Royal Palaces.
Visit our online store: **www.historicroyalpalaces.com** for beautiful gifts inspired by centuries of royal heritage.

*Main picture opposite:*
*The Chapel of St John the Evangelist in the White Tower.*